Meghan O'Gieblyn

INTERIOR STATES

Meghan O'Gieblyn is a writer who was raised and still lives in the Midwest. Her essays have appeared in *Harper's Magazine*, *n+1*, *The Point*, *The New York Times*, *The Guardian*, *The New Yorker*, *Best American Essays 2017*, and the Pushcart Prize anthology. She received a BA in English from Loyola University Chicago and an MFA in Fiction from the University of Wisconsin–Madison. She lives in Madison, Wisconsin, with her husband.

www.meghanogieblyn.com

INTERIOR STATES

INTERIOR STATES

Essays

Meghan O'Gieblyn

ANCHOR BOOKS

A Division of Penguin Random House LLC

New York

AN ANCHOR BOOKS ORIGINAL, OCTOBER 2018

Several pieces first appeared in the following publications: "Pure Michigan"
on *The Awl*; "The End" in the *Boston Review*; "Sniffing Glue" in *Guernica*;
"Exiled" in *Harper's Magazine*; "Maternal Ecstasies" and "On Reading
Updike" in *The Los Angeles Review of Books*; "Ghost in the Cloud" in *n+1*;
"American Niceness" in *The New Yorker*; "A Species of Origins" in *Oxford
American*; "Contemporaries" in *Ploughshares*; "Hell," "The Insane Idea,"
and "Midwestworld" in *The Point*; "Dispatch from Flyover Country" in
The Threepenny Review; and "On Subtlety" in *Tin House*.

Library of Congress Cataloging-in-Publication Data
Names: O'Gieblyn, Meghan, 1982– author.
Title: Interior states : essays / by Meghan O'Gieblyn.
Description: First edition. | New York : Anchor Books, [2018]
Identifiers: LCCN 2018004173 (print) | LCCN 2018004981 (ebook)
Classification: LCC PS3615.G54 (ebook) | LCC PS3615.G54 A6 2018 (print) |
DDC 814/.6—dc23
LC record available at https://lccn.loc.gov/2018004173

Anchor Books Trade Paperback ISBN: 978-0-525-56270-2
eBook ISBN: 978-0-385-54384-2

Book design by Christopher M. Zucker

www.anchorbooks.com

Printed in the United States of America
10 9 8 7 6 5 4 3 2 1

All Americans come from Ohio originally, if only briefly.

—DAWN POWELL

The Middle West is probably a fanatic state of mind. It is, as I see it, an unknown geographic terrain, an amorphous substance, the ghostly interplay of time with space, the cosmic, the psychic, as near to the North Pole as to the Gallup Poll.

—MARGUERITE YOUNG

CONTENTS

PREFACE

One criticism of the personal essay—an old one, though it's been revived with special fervor in recent years—is its tendency toward confession. To some extent, this is simply a matter of lineage. The origins of what we today call "personal writing" can be traced back to Augustine, so it's not coincidental that the genre so frequently reverts to the tenor of the Christian ritual: the divulging of transgressions, the preening need for absolution. In fact, I've often sensed in these complaints about confessional writing an underlying impatience with religion itself and the persistence of its postures in modern life. It is now the twenty-first century, these critics seem to say, and high time we got off our knees and took ownership of our lives.

The faith tradition in which I was raised, evangelical Protestantism, did not practice the rite of private confession. We did not confess; we professed, and we did so publicly. The narrative ritual taken up by our congregation was performed in front of the entire body of fellow believers, a convention called "giving testimony." Most often, your testimony was your life story, though it could also be about a particular struggle or a period of doubt. While confession is typically born of guilt and predicated upon the experience of private catharsis, the testimony had a decidedly communal purpose. The point was not to absolve oneself, but rather to "testify" to the truth of the gospel, using one's story as a form of evidence. Like the courtroom practice from which it derived its name, the idea was that your personal experience was a way of building a case.

Each of the pieces collected in this volume is, in some sense, a testimony, which is to say the essays were spurred not by the need to unburden myself, but rather to connect my experiences to larger conversations and debates. Not all of these essays contain an explicit argument, but each began with a desire to make a claim—or in some cases, to complicate an existing one—coupled with the feeling that my life might serve as a form of evidence. The earliest ones were composed when I was still contending with my loss of faith, and writing them was a way to impose some semblance of order on a world that felt muddled and morally chaotic. Although these early pieces were published in secular magazines, I was writing primarily to evangelicals, trying to elucidate what I saw as a central hypocrisy of the faith I had left: namely, the church's willingness—in its theology on hell, its relationship to science, and its approach to youth culture—to compromise its doctrine in order to remain culturally relevant.

Over the past decade, most of the writing on Christianity in this country has taken the form of obituary. More than one of the magazine editors who published these essays insisted that I acknowledge the 2014 Pew Research study about the rise of the "nones"—young people who claim no religious affiliation—as though to affirm the popular notion that America is leaving behind its superstitious past and treading unwaveringly into the future. Perhaps this is true. But as someone who has traveled that path myself, I can confirm that such journeys are rarely linear or without complications. William James once noted that "the most violent revolutions in an individual's beliefs leave most of his old order standing." In other words, even when a person outwardly denounces a long-standing belief, the architecture of the idea persists and can come to be inhabited by other things. This is as true of cultures as it is of individuals. Some of the essays in this collection examine the ways in which our increasingly secular landscape is still imprinted with the legacy of Christianity. The testimony, as a narrative form, endures in the rooms of twelve-step programs and in contemporary writing about motherhood, which often takes the form of conversion narrative. Meanwhile, the faith's epic story of messianic redemption lives on in the utopic visions of transhumanism and in liberalism's endless arc of progress.

Many of these essays return to questions about history and historical narratives. It is a topic that is difficult these days to avoid—though this is particularly true for those of us who live in the Midwest, which F. Scott Fitzgerald famously called, in *The Great Gatsby*, "the ragged edge of the universe," a place where it's easy to conclude that history is over. Much of my childhood took place outside Detroit, a city that was, during those years, in the process of being reclaimed by the prairie, its downtown haunted by six empty prewar skyscrapers. During the bleakest years of the financial crisis, these rotting cathedrals of commerce became such an unambiguous symbol that some residents proposed their ruins should be preserved as an urban Monument Valley that tourists could visit, as they do the Acropolis of Athens, to witness the collapse of American empire. Of course, this never transpired. Instead, this stretch of downtown has been transformed into a playground for the creative class, a development that has displaced the city's most vulnerable residents and only heightened the sense of historic unreality. Like so many metropolises along the Rust Belt, Detroit has become a hastily drawn caricature of the city it once was, festooned with the signifiers of the manufacturing age (Diego Rivera murals, PBR on tap) that have been drained of any real political and economic significance, while its factories have been reimagined as farm-to-table restaurants and the sleek offices of tech start-ups.

What unites the states of the Midwest—both the ailing and the tenuously "revived"—is a profound loss of telos, the realization that the industries and systems that built the region are no longer tenable. And I suppose what unites these essays is similarly an abiding interest in loss, particularly the loss of direction that occurs after the decline of a doctrine, an economy, or an entire worldview. The notion of "lostness" is, of course, crucial to the genre of Christian testimony, which hinges on the belief that bewilderment, limitation, and doubt can become the source of connections with others and more transcendent sources of meaning.

I feel compelled to mention that I did not set out, in any deliberate way, to write about these topics. In seeing these essays collected, it's difficult to avoid sensing something perverse in the fact that I have returned so obsessively to the religion I spent my early adulthood trying to escape. And while I have written so much about the Midwest, the truth is that I've often felt that I would prefer to live almost anywhere else. I'm not sure how to account for this, except to say that it's a paradox of human nature that the sites of our unhappiness are precisely those that we come to trust most hardily, that we absorb most readily into our identity, and that we defend most vociferously when they come under attack. Like the convert who develops a fondness for the darker moments of her testimony, I have come, through the act of writing, to believe in the virtue of my experience. These essays are a record of that process and contain some provisional attempts to make sense of these preoccupations.

INTERIOR STATES

DISPATCH FROM
FLYOVER COUNTRY

The August before last, my husband and I moved to Muskegon, a town on the scenic and economically depressed west coast of Michigan. We live in a trailer in the woods, one paneled with oak-grained laminate and beneath which a family of raccoons have made their home. There is a small screened-in porch and a large deck that extends over the side of a sand dune. We work there in the mornings beneath the ceiling of broadleaves, teaching our online classes and completing whatever freelance projects we've managed to scrape together that week. Occasionally, I'll try to amuse him by pitching my latest idea for a screenplay. "An out-of-work stuntman leaves Hollywood and becomes an Uber driver," I'll say. "It's about second chances in the sharing economy." We write the kinds of things that return few material rewards; there is no harm in fantasizing. After dinner, we take the trail that runs from the back of the trailer through an aisle of high pines, down the side of the dune to Lake Michigan.

Evenings have been strange this year: hazy, surreal. Ordinarily, Michigan sunsets are like a preview of the apocalypse, a celestial fury of reds and tangerines. But since we moved here, each day expires in white gauze. The evening air grows thick with fog, and as the sun descends toward the water, it grows perfectly round and blood colored, lingering on the horizon like an evil planet. If a paddle-boarder happens to cross the lake, the vista looks exactly like one of those old oil paintings of Hanoi. For a long time, we assumed the haze was smog wafting in from Chicago, or perhaps Milwaukee. But one night, as we walked along the beach, we bumped into a friend of my mother's who told us it was from the California wildfires. She'd heard all about it on the news: smoke from the Sierra Nevada had apparently been carried on an eastern jet stream thousands of miles across the country, all the way to our beach.

"That seems impossible," I said.

"It does seem impossible," she agreed, and the three of us stood there on the shore, staring at the horizon as though, if we looked hard enough, we might glimpse whatever was burning on the far side of the country.

The Midwest is a somewhat slippery notion. It is a region whose existence—whose very name—has always been contingent upon the more fixed and concrete notion of the West. Historically, these interior states were less a destination than a corridor, one that funneled travelers from the East into the vast expanse of the frontier. The great industrial cities of this region—Chicago, Detroit, and St. Louis—were built as "hubs," places where the rivers and the railroads met, where all the goods of the prairie accumulated before being shipped to the exterior states. Today, coastal residents stop here only to change planes, a fact that has solidified our identity as a place to be passed over. To be fair, people who live here seem to prefer it this way. Gift shops along the shores of the Great Lakes sell T-shirts bearing the slogan FLYOVER LIVING. The official motto for the state of Indiana is Crossroads of America. Each time my family passed the state line on childhood road trips, my sisters and I would mock its odd, anti-touristic logic ("Nothing to see here, folks!").

When I was young, my family moved across the borders of these states—from Illinois to Michigan to Wisconsin. My father sold industrial lubricant, an occupation that took us to the kinds of cities that had been built for manufacturing and by the end of the century lay mostly abandoned, covered, like Pompeii, in layers of ash. We lived on the outskirts of these cities, in midcentury bedroom communities, or else beyond them, in subdivisions built atop decimated cornfields. On winter evenings, when the last flush of daylight stretched across the prairie, the only sight for miles was the green-and-white lights of airport runways blinking in the distance like lodestars. We were never far from a freeway, and at night the whistle of trains passing through was as much a part of the soundscape as the wind or the rain. It is like this anywhere you go in the Midwest. It is the sound of transit, of things passing through. People who grew up here tend to tune it out, but if you stop and actually listen, it can be disarming. On some nights, it's easy to imagine that it is the sound of a more profound shifting, as though the entire landscape of this region—the North Woods, the tallgrass prairies, the sand dunes, and the glacial moraines—is itself fluid and impermanent.

It's difficult to live here without developing an existential dizziness, a sense that the rest of the world is moving while you remain still. I spent most of my twenties in South Chicago, in an apartment across from a hellscape of coal-burning plants that ran on grandfather clauses and churned out smoke blacker than the night sky. To live there during the digital revolution was like existing in an anachronism. When I opened my windows in summer, soot blew in with the breeze; I swept piles of it off my floor, which left my hands blackened like a scullery maid's. I often thought that Dickens's descriptions of industrial England might have aptly described twenty-first-century Chicago: "It was a town of machinery and tall chimneys, out of which interminable serpents of smoke trailed themselves for ever and ever, and never got uncoiled." Far from the blat of the city, there was another world, one depicted on television and in the pages of magazines—a nirvana of sprawling green parks and the distant silence of wind turbines. Billboards glowed above the streets like portals into another world, one where everything was reduced to clean and essential lines. YOU ARE BEAUTIFUL read one of them, its product unmentioned or unclear. Another featured a blue sky marked with cumulus clouds and the words IMAGINE PEACE.

I still believed during those years that I would end up in New York—or perhaps in California. I never had any plans for how to get there. I truly believed I would "end up" there, swept by that force of nature that funneled each harvest to the exterior states and carried young people off along with it. Instead, I found work as a cocktail waitress at a bar downtown, across from the state prison. The regulars were graying men who sat impassively at the bar each night, reading the *Tribune* in silence. The nature of my job, according to my boss, was to be an envoy of feminine cheer in that dark place, and so I occasionally wandered over to offer some chipper comment on the headlines—

"Looks like the stimulus package is going to pass"—a task that was invariably met with a cascade of fatalism.

"You think any of that money's going to make it to Chicago?"

"They should make Wall Street pay for it," someone quipped.

"Nah, that would be too much like right."

Any news of emerging technology was roundly dismissed as unlikely. If I mentioned self-driving cars, or 3-D printers, one of the men would hold up his cell phone and say, "They can't even figure out how to get us service south of Van Buren."

For a long time, I mistook this for cynicism. In reality, it is something more like stoicism, a resistance to excitement that is native to this region. The longer I live here, the more I detect it in myself. It is less disposition than habit, one that comes from tuning out the fashions and revelations of the coastal cities, which have nothing to do with you, just as you learned as a child to ignore those local boosters who proclaimed, year after year, that your wasted Rust Belt town was on the cusp of revival. Some years ago, the Detroit Museum of Contemporary Art installed on its western exterior a neon sign that read EVERYTHING IS GOING TO BE ALRIGHT. For several months, this message brightened the surrounding blight and everyone spoke of it as a symbol of hope. Then the installation was changed to read: NOTHING IS GOING TO BE ALRIGHT. They couldn't help themselves, I guess. To live here is to develop a wariness of all forms of unqualified optimism; it is to know that progress comes in fits and starts; that whatever promise the future holds, its fruits may very well pass by, on their way to somewhere else.

My husband and I live just up the hill from the grounds of a Bible camp where I spent the summers of my childhood, a place called Maranatha. People in town assume the name is Native American, but it is in fact an Aramaic phrase that means "Come, Lord," and which appears in the closing sentences of the New Testament. The apostolic fathers once spoke the phrase as a prayer, and it was repeated by people of faith throughout the centuries, a mantra to fill God's millennia-long silence. When the camp was built in the early years of the last century, a more ominous English formulation—"The Lord Is Coming"—was carved into the cedar walls of the Tabernacle. Everyone is still waiting.

From Memorial Day to Labor Day, the grounds are overrun with evangelical families who come from all over the Midwest to spend their summer vacations on the beach. They stay for weeks at a time in the main lodge, and some stay for the whole summer in cottages built on stilts atop what is the largest collection of freshwater dunes in the world. My parents own one of these cottages; so do my grandparents. Each year a representative from the Department of Natural Resources comes out to warn them that the dunes are eroding and the houses will one day slide into the lake—prophecies that go unheeded. Everyone plants more dune grass and prays for a few more years. I once pointed out to my mother that there is, in fact, a biblical parable about the foolish man who builds his house on sand, but she chided me for my pedantic literalism. "That parable," she said, "is about having a foundational faith."

We moved here because we love this part of Michigan and because I have family here. Also because it's cheap to live here and we're poor. We've lost track of the true reason. Or rather, the foremost reasons and the incidental ones are easy to confuse. Before, we were in Madison, Wisconsin, where we were teaching college writing and juggling other part-time jobs. As more of this work migrated online, location became negotiable. We have the kind of career people like to call "flexible," meaning we buy our own health insurance, work in our underwear, and are taxed like a small business. Sometimes we fool ourselves into believing that we've outsmarted the system, that we've harnessed the plucky spirit of those DIY blogs that applaud young couples for turning a toolshed or a teardrop camper into a studio apartment, as though economic instability were the great crucible of American creativity.

On Saturday nights, the camp hosts a concert, and my husband and I occasionally walk down to the Tabernacle to listen to whatever band has been bused in from Nashville. Neither of us are believers, but we enjoy the music. The bands favor gospel standards, a blend of highlands ballads and Gaither-style revivalism. The older generation here includes a contingent of retired missionaries. Many of them are widows, women who spent their youth carrying the gospel to the Philippines or the interior of Ecuador, and after the service, they smile faintly at me as they pass by our pew, perhaps sensing a family resemblance. Occasionally, one of them will grip my forearm and say, "Tell me who you are." The response to this question is "I'm Colleen's daughter." Or, if that fails to register: "I'm Paul and Marilyn's granddaughter." It is unnerving to identify oneself in this way. My husband once noted that it harkens back to the origins of surnames, to the clans of feudal times who identified villagers by patronymic epithets. John's son became Johnson, et cetera. To do so now is to see all the things that constitute a modern identity—all your quirks and accomplishments—rendered obsolete.

This is among the many reasons why young people leave these states. When you live in close proximity to your parents and aging relatives, it's impossible to forget that you too will grow old and die. It's the same reason, I suspect, that people are made uncomfortable by the specter of open landscapes, why the cornfields and empty highways of the heartland inspire so much angst. There was a time when people spoke of such vistas as metaphors for opportunity—"expand your horizons"—a convention, I suppose, that goes back to the days of the frontier. Today, opportunity is the province of cities, and the view here signals not possibility but visible constraints. To look out at the expanse of earth, scraped clean of novelty and distraction, is to remember in a very real sense what lies at the end of your own horizon.

Many of our friends who grew up here now live in Brooklyn, where they are at work on "book-length narratives." Another contingent has moved to the Bay Area and made a fortune there. Every year or so, these West Coasters travel back to Michigan and call us up for dinner or drinks, occasions they use to educate us on the inner workings of the tech industry. They refer to the companies they work for in the first person plural, a habit of the rest of the country I have yet to acculturate to. Occasionally, they lapse into the utopian, speaking of robotics ordinances and brain-computer interfaces and the mystical, labyrinthine channels of capital, conveying it all with the fervency of pioneers on a civilizing mission. Being lectured quickly becomes dull, and so my husband and I, to amuse ourselves, will sometimes play the rube: "So what, exactly, is a venture capitalist?" we'll say. Or "Gosh, it sounds like science fiction." I suppose we could tell them the truth—that nothing they're proclaiming is news; that the boom and bustle of the coastal cities, like the smoke from those California wildfires, liberally wafts over the rest of the country. But that seems a bit rude. We are, after all, midwesterners.

Here, work is work and money is money, and nobody speaks of these things as though they were spiritual movements or expressions of one's identity. In college, I waitressed at a chain restaurant, the kind of place that played Smash Mouth on satellite and cycled through twenty gallons of ranch dressing a week. One day, it was announced that all employees—from management to dish crew—would hereafter be referred to as "partners." It was a diktat from corporate. Everyone found this so absurd that all of us, including the assistant managers, refused to say the word without a cartoonish, cowboy twang ("Howdy, pard'ner"), robbing it of its intended purpose, which was, of course, to erase the appearance of hierarchy. This has always struck me as indicative of a local political disposition, one that cannot be hoodwinked into euphemism. When you live at the center of the American machine, it's impossible to avoid speaking of mechanics.

Winters here are dark and brutal. On weekends, my husband and I will drive into town, where there are five or six restaurants that have different names but identical menus. Each serves fried perch and whitefish sandwiches, plus a salad section that boasts an Epcot-like *tour du monde*: Chinese salad, taco salad, Thai chicken salad, Southwest salad. In Michigan, they still—thankfully—believe in iceberg lettuce, or as one menu has it: "crisp, cold iceberg lettuce." At the more "high-end" Muskegon restaurants, you can order something called a wedge salad, which is a quarter of a head of iceberg covered in tomatoes, bacon bits, and what appears to be—but is not, actually—a profane amount of blue cheese *and* French dressings. "Oh shit," my husband said the first time I ordered one in his presence. "They forgot your dressing." Of course, anyone familiar with iceberg heads knows that they are baroquely layered and dense; you truly do need all that dressing. People in Michigan understand these things.

But even here, in Muskegon, there are headwinds of change.

At the farmers market, there is now one stand—the only place in town—that sells organic whole-bean coffee and makes pour-overs while you wait. The owner, Dave, wears white Oakleys and speaks as though he learned about the artisanal revolution at a corporate convention. "The best places are those that have five things on the menu," he tells us. "Don't make it complicated, man. Just make it good." Across the street from the market is a farm-to-table restaurant where you can order sous vide octopus and duck tortellini. A sister restaurant recently opened next door, the Whistle Punk, a sparse stone-oven pizza joint whose ingredient list, scrawled on brown paper, lists maque choux and Swiss chard sourced from local farms. A "Whistle Punk," reads the restaurant's website, is "an affectionate term given to the newest member of a logging camp."

Muskegon is, in fact, an old logging hub, a mill town once known as the "Lumber Queen of the World." It's tempting to see in such gestures evidence of the hinterland becoming conscious, an entire region rising up to lay claim to its roots. It would be easier to believe this if the coveted look in *Brooklyn Magazine*, about ten years ago, were not called "the lumberjack."

There are places in the Midwest that are considered oases—cities that lie within the coordinates of the region but do not technically belong there. The model in this mode is Madison, Wisconsin, the so-called Berkeley of the Midwest. The comparison stems from the 1960s, when students stormed the campus to protest the Vietnam War. The campus mall is still guarded by foreboding Brutalist structures that were, according to local lore, built during that era as an intimidation tactic. I taught in one of these buildings when I was in graduate school. The other

TAs complained about them, claiming they got headaches from the lack of sunlight and the maze of asymmetrical halls. I found them beautiful, despite their politics. During my first day of class, I would walk my students outside to show them the exterior. I noted how the walls canted away from the street, evoking a fortress. I pointed out the narrow windows, impossible to smash with rocks. "Buildings," I told them, "can be arguments. Everything you see is an argument." The students were first-semester freshmen, bright and bashful farm kids who had come to this great metropolis—this Athens of the prairie—with the wholesome desire to learn.

Those buildings, like all the old buildings in town, were constantly under threat of demolition. Many of the heavy masonry structures had already been torn down to make way for condo high-rises, built to house the young employees of Epic—a healthcare software company that bills itself as the "Google of the Midwest." The corporate headquarters, located just outside town, was a legendary place that boasted all the hallmarks of Menlo Park excess: a gourmet cafeteria with chefs poached from five-star restaurants, an entire wing decorated to resemble Hogwarts. During the years I lived in Madison, the city was flush with new money. A rash of artisanal shops and restaurants broke out across town, each of them channeling the spirit of the prairie and its hardworking, industrial ethos. The old warehouses were refurbished into posh restaurants whose names evoked the surrounding countryside (Graze, Harvest). They were the kinds of places where rye whiskeys were served on bars made of reclaimed barn wood, and veal was cooked by chefs whose forearms were tattooed with Holsteins. Most of the factories in town had been turned into breweries, or the kind of coffee shops that resembled an eighteenth-century workshop—

all the baristas in butcher aprons and engaged in what appeared to be chemistry experiments with espresso.

Meanwhile, the actual industry, unhidden in the middle of the downtown, looked as though it had never been used. There were gleaming aluminum silos and emissionless brick chimneys. In the prairie stockyards near my apartment, blue railroad cars were lined up like children's toys. Beyond the fences, giant coils of yellow industrial hose glimmered in the early morning light, as beautiful as Monet's haystacks. I doubt that any visitor would see in such artifacts the signs of progress, but when you live for any period in the Midwest, you become sensitive to the subtle process by which industry gives way to commerce, and utility to aesthetics.

Each spring arrived with the effulgent bloom of the farmers market. The sidewalks around the capitol became flush with white flowers, heirloom eggs, and little pots of honey, and all the city came out in linen and distressed denim. There were food carts parked on the sidewalk, and a string quartet playing "Don't Stop Believing," and my husband and I, newly in love, sitting on the steps of the capitol. We kept our distance from the crowds, preferring to watch from afar. He pointed out that the Amish men selling cherry pies were indistinguishable from the students busking in straw hats and suspenders. It was strange, all these paeans to the pastoral. In the coastal cities, throwbacks of this sort are regarded as a romantic reaction against the sterile exigencies of urban life. But Madison was smack in the middle of the heartland. You could, in theory, drive five miles out of town and find yourself in the great oblivion of corn.

In the early days of our relationship, we were always driving out to those parts, spurred by some vague desire to see the limits of the land—or perhaps to distinguish the simulacrum from

the real. We would download albums from our teen years—
Night on the Sun, Either/Or—and drive east on the expressway
until the sprawl of subdivisions gave way to open land. If there
was a storm in the forecast, we'd head out to the farmland of
Black Earth, flying past the crop fields with all the windows
down, the backseat fluttering with unread newspapers as light-
ning forked across the horizon.

Madison was utopia for a certain kind of midwesterner: the
Baptist boy who grew up reading Wittgenstein, the farm lass
who secretly dreamed about the girl next door. It should have
been such a place for me as well. Instead, I came to find the live
bluegrass outside the co-op insufferable. I developed a physical
allergy to NPR. Sitting in a bakery one morning, I heard the
opening theme of *Morning Edition* drift in from the kitchen and
started scratching my arms as though contracting a rash. My
husband tried to get me to articulate what it was that bothered
me, but I could never come up with the right adjective. Self-
satisfied? Self-congratulatory? I could never get past aesthetics. On the way home from teaching my night class, I would
unwind by listening to a fundamentalist preacher who delivered exegeses on the Pentateuch and occasionally lapsed into
fire and brimstone. The drive was long, and I would slip into
something like a trance state, failing to register the import of
the message but calmed nonetheless by the familiar rhythm of
conviction.

Over time, I came to dread the parties and potlucks. Most
of the people we knew had spent time on the coasts, or had
come from there, or were frequently traveling from one to the
other, and the conversation was always about what was happening elsewhere: what people were listening to in Williamsburg,
or what everyone was wearing at Coachella. A sizeable portion
of the evening was devoted to the plots of premium TV dramas.

Occasionally, there were long arguments about actual ideas, but they always crumbled into semantics. "What do you mean by *duty?*" someone would say. Or: "It all depends on your definition of *morality.*" At the end of these nights, I would get into the car with the first throb of a migraine, saying that we didn't have any business discussing anything until we could, all of us, articulate a coherent ideology. It seemed to me then that we suffered from the fundamental delusion that we had elevated ourselves above the rubble of hinterland ignorance—that fair trade coffee and Orange You Glad It's Vegan? cake had somehow redeemed us of our sins. All of us had, like the man in the parable, built our houses on sand.

A couple weeks ago, there was a mass baptism in Lake Michigan. There is one at the end of each summer, though I haven't attended one in years. It was a warm night, and so my husband and I walked down to watch, along with my mother, my sister, and her two-year-old daughter. The haze was thick that evening, and it wasn't until we were nearly upon the crowd that we could see it in its entirety: hundreds of people standing along the shore, barefoot like refugees in the sand. Out in the water, a pastor stood waist-deep with a line of congregants waiting their turn in the shallows. Farther down, there was another pastor standing in the lake with another line of congregants, and even farther down, near the rocks of the channel, a third stood with yet another line of people. The water was so gray and still, the evening air so windless, that you could hear the pastors' voices as they recited the sacramental formula: "Buried with Christ in baptism, raised to walk in the newness of life." Whenever someone emerged from the water, everyone on the beach cheered and clapped as the congregant waded back through the mist like a ghost, their clothes suddenly thin and weighed down with water.

My mother saw someone she knew in the crowd and walked over to say hello. A small drone flew over the water, hovering over each of the pastors and then darted along the shoreline. My sister pointed it out. It must be filming, we decided. The beach was clean from a recent storm, empty except for some stray pieces of driftwood, bleached white and hewn smooth as whale bones. The seagulls were circling in frantic patterns, as though trying to warn us. Usually they glide over the beach in elegant arabesques, but there was no wind on this night, and they flapped like bats, trying to stay afloat.

The whole scene seemed to me like a Bruegel painting, a sweeping portrait of community life already distilled by time. I imagined scholars examining it many years in the future, trying to decipher its rituals and iconography. There was something beautiful in how the pastor laid his hands over the congregant's face, covering her hand with his own, something beautiful in the bewildered look on the congregant's face when she emerged from the water. Although I no longer espouse this faith, it's hard to deny the mark it has left on me. It is a conviction that lies beneath the doctrine and theology, a kind of bone-marrow knowledge that the Lord is coming; that he has always been coming, which is the same as saying that he will never come; that each of us must find a way to live with this absence and our own, earthly limitations.

The crowd erupted again in cheers. I was watching my niece run through the surf, watching my sister pretend to chase her. Each time the crowd cheered, she threw her hands above her head, as though it were for her. The drone made its way toward us, descended and hovered there, just above the water.

"That's unsettling," I said. The machine was idling above

the water, appearing to stare us down. It was close enough that I could see the lens of its camera, a red light going on and off, as though winking at us.

"It knows we're not believers," my husband whispered.

"Let's go," I said. We made our way into the crowd, hoping to disappear within it. Everyone was dressed in brightly colored shirts and smelled of damp cotton. We passed my mother, who was laughing. The voices of the pastors carried irregularly across the water, and once we were deep in the crowd, their incantations seemed to overlap, as though it were one voice, rippling in a series of echoes. "Buried with Christ . . . Raised to walk in the newness . . ." Things were ending and beginning again, just as everything is always ending and always beginning, and standing there amid the sea of people, I was reminded that it might not go on like this forever. We made our way to the shore, where the crowd thinned out and the sand was firm with water, and beyond the fog there appeared, on the horizon, the faintest trace of a sunset.

2016, *The Threepenny Review*

HELL

A couple of years ago, a Chicago-based corporate identity consultant named Chris Herron gave himself the ultimate challenge: rebrand hell. It was half gag, half self-promotion, but Herron took the project seriously, considering what it would require in the travel market for a place like hell to become a premier destination. The client was the Hell Office of Travel and Tourism (HOTT), which supposedly hired Herron in the wake of a steady decline in visitors caused by "a stale and unfocused brand strategy." After toying with some playfully sinful logos—the kind you might find on skater/goth products—Herron decided that what the locale needed to stay competitive in the afterlife industry was a complete brand overhaul. The new hell would feature no demons or devils, no tridents or lakes of fire. The brand name was rendered in a lowercase, bubbly blue font, a word mark designed to evoke "instant accessibility and comfort." The slogan—which had evolved from "Abandon Hope All Ye Who Enter Here" (1819) to "When You've Been Bad, We've Got It Good" (1963) to "Give In to Temptation" (2001)—would be "Simply Heavenly." The joke was posted as a "case study" on Herron's personal website and quickly went viral in the marketing blogosphere—a testament to the power of effective branding.

I grew up in an evangelical community that wasn't versed in these kinds of sales-pitch seductions. My family belonged to a dwindling Baptist congregation in southeast Michigan, where Sunday mornings involved listening to our pastor unabashedly preach something akin to the 1819 version of hell—a real diabolical place where sinners suffered for all eternity. In the 1990s, when most kids my age were performing interpretive dances to "The Greatest Love of All" and receiving enough gold stars to fill a minor galaxy, my peers and I sat in Sunday school each week, memorizing scripture like 1 Peter 5:8: "Be self-controlled and alert. Your enemy the devil prowls around like a roaring lion looking for someone to devour."*

I was too young and sheltered to recognize that this worldview was anachronistic. Even now as an adult, it's difficult for me to hear scholars like Elaine Pagels refer to Satan as "an antiquarian relic of a superstitious age," or to come across an aside, in a magazine article, that claims the Western world stopped believing in a literal hell *during the Enlightenment*. My parents often attributed chronic sins like alcoholism or adultery to

* I think evangelicals are under the impression that any scriptural passage with an animal reference is kid-friendly. In fact, this verse once inspired my Christian camp counselors to have our second-grade class sing a version of the doo-wop classic "The Lion Sleeps Tonight" as "The Devil Sleeps Tonight," which we performed for our parents, cheerily snapping our fingers and chanting *"awimbawe, awimbawe,"* etc.

"spiritual warfare" (as in, "Let's remember to pray for Larry, who's struggling with spiritual warfare") and taught me and my siblings that evil was a real force that was in all of us. Our dinner conversations sounded like something out of a Hawthorne novel.

According to Christian doctrine, all human beings, believers included, are sinners by nature. This essentially means that no one can get through life without committing at least one moral transgression. In the eleventh century, Saint Anselm of Canterbury defined original sin as "privation of the righteousness that every man ought to possess." Although the "saved" are forgiven of their sins, they're never cured. Even Paul the apostle wrote, "Christ Jesus came into the world to save sinners—*of whom I am the worst*" [emphasis mine]. According to this view, hell isn't so much a penitentiary for degenerates as it is humanity's default destination. But there's a way out through accepting Christ's atonement, which, in the Protestant tradition, involves saying the sinner's prayer. For contemporary evangelicals, it's solely this act that separates the sheep from the goats. I've heard more than one believer argue that Mother Teresa is in hell for not saying this prayer, while Jeffrey Dahmer, who supposedly accepted Christ weeks before his murder, is in heaven.

I got saved when I was five years old. I have no memory of my conversion, but apparently my mom led me through the prayer, which involves confessing that you are a sinner and inviting Jesus into your heart. She might have told me about hell that night, or maybe I already knew it existed. Having a frank family talk about eternity was seen as a responsibility not unlike warning your kids about drugs or unprotected sex. It was uncomfortable, but preferable to the possible consequences of not doing so. Many Protestants believe that once a person is saved, it's impossible for her to lose her eternal security—even if she renounces her faith—so there's an urgency to catch kids before they start to ask questions. Most of the kids I grew up with were saved before they'd lost their baby teeth.

For those who'd managed to slip between the cracks, the scare tactics started in earnest around middle school. The most memorable was *Without Reservation*, a thirty-minute video that I was lucky enough to see half a dozen times over the course of my teens. The film (which begins with the disclaimer: "The following is an abstract representation of actual events and realities") has both the production quality and the setup of a driver's ed video: five teens are driving home from a party, after much merrymaking, when their car gets broadsided by a semi. There's a brief montage of sirens and police radio voice-overs. Then it cuts to four of the kids, Bill, Ken, John, and Mary, waking up in the car, which is mysteriously suspended in space. Below them is a line hundreds of people long, leading up to a man with white hair, stationed behind a giant IBM. When a person reaches the front of the line, this man (who's probably supposed to be God or Saint Peter, but looks uncannily like Bob Barker) types the person's name into a DOS-like database, bringing up their photo, cause of death, and one of two messages: "Reservation Confirmed" or "Reservation Not Confirmed." He then instructs them to step to either the left or the right.

At this point, it's clear that this isn't a film about the dangers of operating under the influence. The kids begin to realize that they're dead. One of them, Bill, a Christian, uneasily explains to the others that what they're seeing is a judgment line, at which point Mary loses it, shaking uncontrollably and sobbing, "I want to go back! Why can't we all just go back!" The rest of the film consists of a long sequence showing their memorial service, back on Earth, during which some kind of school administrator speaks in secular platitudes about death being a place of safety and peace—a eulogy that is interspliced with shots of Ken, John, and Mary learning that their reservation is "not confirmed," then being led down a red-lit hall and violently pushed into caged elevators. The last shot of them is in these cells—Mary curled in the fetal position, Ken and John pounding on the chain-link walls—as they descend into darkness. There's a little vignette at the end in which the fifth, surviving, passenger gets saved in the school cafeteria, but by that point I was always too shell-shocked to find it redemptive.

It would be difficult to overstate the effect this film had on my adolescent psyche. Lying in bed at night, I replayed the elevator scene over and over in my head, imagining what fate lay in store for those kids and torturing myself with the possibility that I might be one of the unconfirmed. What if I had missed a crucial part of the prayer? Or what if God's computer got some kind of celestial virus and my name was erased? When you get saved young, when you have no life transformation—no rugged past to turn from—the prayer itself carries real power, like a hex.*

This anxiety was exacerbated by the fact that, around junior high, youth leaders began urging us to "re-invite" Christ into our lives. They insinuated that those of us who had been saved

---

* At one point during my early teens, before I understood the concept of eternal security, it occurred to me that if I could ask Jesus into my heart, I could just as easily ask him to leave. Once this fear lodged itself in my brain, it became impossible not to think the prayer "Jesus, go out of my heart," the way it's impossible not to visualize a purple hippopotamus once someone tells you not to. For weeks, I found myself mentally replaying this heresy, then immediately correcting it with the proper salvation prayer, all the while terrified that something would happen to me (a car accident, a brain aneurysm) in the seconds in between, while I was technically unsaved.

early might not have *actually* been saved—particularly if we were just repeating the formula obediently after our parents. Some said the childhood prayers had been provisional, a safety net until we reached the age of accountability (traditionally believed to be twelve). Apparently, the words weren't enough— you had to mean them, and, at least to some extent, you had to live them. Good works couldn't get you into heaven, but if your life showed no sign of the Holy Spirit working in you, this was a hint that you might not have been completely genuine when you asked Jesus into your life.

One of the most obvious ways of living your faith was through evangelism. I recently rewatched *Without Reservation* and realized that when I was a kid I'd totally missed the intended message. The film was not a scare tactic meant to trick teens into becoming Christians; it was very clearly designed for the already saved, a dramatized pep talk urging us to get the word out about hell to our non-Christian friends. The most dramatic sequence of the film (apart from the elevator scene) is when John, before being carried off to hell, asks Bill, the believer, why he never said anything about eternal damnation. "We rode home from practice together every day," he pleads. "We talked about a lot of stuff, but we never talked about this." Bill can only offer feeble excuses like "I thought you weren't interested!" and "I thought there was more time!"

That this message never got across to me might have had something to do with the fact that, as a homeschooled junior high student, I actually didn't know any unbelievers. In my mind, the "lost" consisted of a motley minority of animal-worshipping tribesmen, Michael Jackson, Madonna, and our Catholic neighbors. It wasn't until I started going to public high school that I began to feel a gnawing guilt, spurred by the realization that my evolution-touting biology teacher, or the girl who sat next to me in study hall reading *The Satanic Bible*, was going to spend eternity suffering. Despite this, I never got up the courage to share my faith. Part of it was surely a lack of personal conviction. But I was also becoming aware that sharing the gospel message—which depends on convincing a person he's a sinner in need of God's grace—sounded remarkably offensive and self-righteous. Our pastor always said that we needed to speak about hell in a spirit of love, but he clearly didn't know what it was like to be a teenager in the 1990s. I went to a high school that didn't publish the honor roll for fear of hurting those who weren't on it. The most popular yearbook quote among my graduating class was Tupac's "Only God can judge me." And most of those kids didn't even believe in God.

In retrospect, *Without Reservation* was likely a last-ditch effort, one of the church's final attempts to convince the emerging generation of the need to speak candidly about eternity. Over the course of my teenage years, Christians began to slip into awkward reticence about the doctrine of damnation. Believers still talked about the afterlife, but the language was increasingly euphemistic and vague. People who rejected Jesus were "eternally separated from God." We were saved not from an infinity of torment, but from "the bondage of sin." Back then, nobody in ministry had the hubris—nor, probably, the sophistication—to rebrand hell à la Chris Herron. Rather, hell was relegated to the margins of the gospel message, the fine print on the eternal-life warranty.

In the King James Bible, the English word "hell" serves as the translation of four different Greek and Hebrew terms. The Old Testament refers exclusively to Sheol, the traditional Hebrew underworld, a place of stillness in which both the righteous and the unrighteous wander in shadows. There's no fiery torment, no wailing or gnashing of teeth. The devil had not yet been invented (though Satan, a trickster angel with whom he would later be conflated, pops up now and then). Sinners seem remarkably off the hook—so much so that Job laments that the wicked "spend their days in prosperity and in peace they go down to Sheol." For many of these writers, the word "Sheol" simply denotes its literal translation, "grave," or unconscious death. The psalmist prays, "For in death there is no remembrance of thee: in Sheol who shall give thee thanks?"

In the New Testament, several writers refer to this place under its Greek name, Hades. There are also a number of passages about Gehenna, literally "the Valley of Hinnom," which was a real area outside Jerusalem that served as the city dump. Fires burned there constantly, to incinerate the garbage; it was also a place where the bodies of criminals were burned. The Jewish rabbinical tradition envisioned Gehenna as a purgatorial place of atonement for the ungodly. This is the word Jesus uses when he gives the hyperbolic command that one should cut off the hand that is causing one to sin: "It is better for you to enter into life maimed, rather than having your two hands to go into Gehenna, into the unquenchable fire." Another Greek term, Tartarus, appears only once, when the author of 2 Peter writes about the angel rebellion that took place before the creation of the world. Drawing from the Greek myth of the Olympians overthrowing the Titans, he recounts how Lucifer and his allies were cast out of heaven into Tartarus. In the *Aeneid*, Virgil describes Tartarus as a place of torment guarded by the Hydra and surrounded by a river of fire to prevent the escape of condemned souls. Except in the 2 Peter version, there are no human souls there, just fallen angels.

The most dramatic descriptions of hell come from the strain

of apocalyptic literature that runs through the New Testament, as well as from the Old Testament prophets. Apocalypticism was a worldview that arose during the sixth century BCE, when Israel was under Babylonian domination. It involved the belief that the present era, which was ruled by evil, would soon give way to a new age here on Earth in which God would restore justice and all evildoers would be punished. The authors of Daniel and Ezekiel were apocalyptists—so was John of Patmos, the author of Revelation. It's these authors who provide us with passages such as this: "They will be tormented with burning sulfur in the presence of the holy angels and of the Lamb. And the smoke of their torment will rise for ever and ever." It's worth noting that this was a belief system born out of persecution. The book of Daniel was written in response to the oppressive monarch Antiochus Epiphanes; the book of Revelation came about during the rule of Domitian, who had Christians burned, crucified, and fed to wild animals. As Nietzsche noted in *On the Genealogy of Morals*, these passages are essentially revenge fantasies, written by people who'd suffered horrible injustices and had no hope of retribution in this life. In fact, many of the fantastical beasts that populate these books were meant to represent contemporary rulers like Nero or Antiochus.

I didn't learn any of this at church. As a kid, it never occurred to me that Solomon and Daniel had drastically different views about the afterlife. Christian theology, as it has developed over the centuries, has functioned like a narrative gloss, smoothing the irregular collection of biblical literature into a cohesive story written by a single, divine author. Secular scholars refer to this as "the myth," the story that depicts all of human history as an epic of redemption. Drawing from his background as a Pharisee, the apostle Paul connected Hebrew scripture to the life of Christ. Just as sin entered the world through one man, Adam, so the world can be redeemed by the death of one man. As time went on, Satan, Lucifer, and Beelzebub were consolidated into a single entity, the personification of all evil. Likewise Sheol, Gehenna, Hades, and Tartarus came to be understood as physical representations of the darkest place in the universe. By the time the King James Bible was published in the seventeenth century, each of these words was translated as simply "hell."

The various depictions of hell over the centuries tend to mirror the earthly landscape of their age. Torture entered the conception of hell in the second century, when Christians were subjected to sadistic public spectacles. Roman interrogation methods included red-hot metal rods, whips, and the rack—a contraption that distended limbs from their joints. The non-canonical Apocalypse of Peter, a product of this era, features a fierce and sadistic hell in which people are blinded by fire and mangled by wild beasts. Dante's *Divine Comedy* has traces of the feudal landscape of fourteenth-century Europe. Lower hell is dramatized as a walled city with towers, ramparts, bridges, and moats; fallen angels guard the citadel like knights. The Jesuits, who rose to prominence during a time of mass immigration and urban squalor, envisioned an inferno of thousands of diseased bodies "pressed together like grapes in a wine-press." It was a claustrophobic hell without latrines, and part of the torture was the human stench.

Today, biblical literalists believe hell exists outside of time and space, in some kind of spiritual fifth dimension. Contemporary evangelical churches don't display paintings or stained glass renderings of hell. It's no longer a popular subject of art. If hell shows up at all these days, it's in pop culture, where it appears as either satirically gaudy—like animated Hieronymus Bosch—or else eerily banal. In *The Far Side*, Satan and his minions are depicted as bored corporate drones who deal with the scourge of the postindustrial Earth. ("There's an insurance salesman here," Satan's secretary says. "Should I admit him or tell him to go to Heaven?") One of the most popular diabolical archetypes in recent years has been the effete Satan. He shows up in episodes of *The Simpsons* and appears in Tenacious D videos, whining about the fine print of the Demon Code. He makes cameos in *South Park*, where he's usually involved in petty domestic squabbles with his boyfriend, Saddam Hussein. Satan has become an unwelcome nuisance, an impotent archetype occasionally dragged out for a good laugh. In an episode of *Saturday Night Live* from 1998, Garth Brooks plays a struggling musician who tries to sell his soul to the devil for a hit song, only to find that Satan (Will Ferrell) is an even more pathetic songwriter than he. When Satan finally gives up and asks if he can leave, Garth shows him out and tells him to lock the door behind him.

Although the sermons of my childhood were often set against the backdrop of hell, I wasn't introduced to the theological doctrine of damnation until I enrolled at Moody Bible Institute at the age of eighteen. Known within evangelical circles as the "West Point of Christian Service," Moody is one of the most conservative Christian colleges in the country. When I was there, students weren't allowed to dance, watch movies, or be alone in a room with a member of the opposite sex. The campus was downtown, occupying a purgatorial no-man's-land between the luxurious Gold Coast and the Cabrini-Green housing projects, but most of the students rarely left campus. The buildings were connected by subterranean tunnels, so it was possible to spend months, particularly in the winter, going from class to the dining hall to the dorms without ever stepping outside. We spent our free time quizzing one another on Greek homework, debating predestination over soft-serve ice cream at the student center, and occasionally indulging in some doctrinal humor (Q: What do you call an Arminian whale? A: Free Willy).

Ideologically, Moody is a peculiar place. Despite the atmosphere of serious scholarship, the institute is theologically conservative, meaning that we studied scripture not as a historic artifact, but as the Word of God. Most of the professors thought the world was created in six days. Nearly all of them believed in a literal hell.* One of the most invidious tasks of the conservative theologian is to explain how a loving God can allow people to suffer for all of eternity. God is omnipotent, and Paul claims it is his divine will that all people should be saved—yet hell

---

* There's a widespread misconception that biblical literalism is facile and mindless, but the doctrine I was introduced to at Moody was every bit as complicated and arcane as Marxist theory or post-structuralism. There were students at the institute who got in fierce debates about infralapsarianism versus supralapsarianism (don't ask) and considered devoting their lives to pneumatology (the study of the Holy Spirit). In many ways, Christian literalism is even *more* complicated than liberal brands of theology because it involves the sticky task of reconciling the overlay myth—the story of redemption—with a wildly inconsistent body of scripture. This requires consummate parsing of Old Testament commands, distinguishing the universal (e.g., thou shalt not kill) from those particular to the Mosaic law that are no longer relevant after the death of Christ (e.g., a sexually violated woman must marry her rapist). It requires making the elaborate case that the Song of Solomon, a book of Hebrew erotica that managed to wangle its way into the canon, is a metaphor about Christ's love for the church, and that the starkly nihilistic book of Ecclesiastes is a representation of the hopelessness of life without God.

exists. Although I'd never given this problem much thought before taking freshman systematic theology, it clearly posed a thorny paradox. In layman's terms, the argument our professors gave us went something like this: God is holy by nature and cannot allow sin into his presence (that is, into heaven). He loves all humans—in fact, he loves them so much that he gave them free will, so that they could choose to refuse salvation. In this way, people essentially condemned themselves to hell. God wasn't standing over the lake of fire, laughing uproariously while casting souls into the flames. Hell was simply the dark side of the universe, the yin to God's yang, something that must exist for there to be universal justice.

There were still a number of problems with this formulation, but for the most part I was willing to suspend my disbelief and trust that God's ways were higher than my own. What bothered me were the numbers. Freshman year, every student was required to take a seminar called Christian Missions, a history of international evangelism that was taught by Dr. Elizabeth Lightbody, a six-foot-three retired missionary to the Philippines who sported a topiary of grayish-blond curls, dressed in garish wool suits, and smiled so incessantly that she appeared a bit maniacal. During the first week of class, we watched a video that claimed there were currently 2.8 billion people among "the unreached"—that is, people who had never heard the gospel. Dr. Lightbody, like the rest of the faculty, adhered to exclusivism, the belief that only those who professed faith in Jesus Christ can be saved (as opposed to pluralism, the belief that people of all religions will be saved, regardless of the name they use for God). Jesus said that "no man comes to the Father, except through me," and we had to take this word for word as the truth, meaning it included those who had no idea who Jesus was.* Technically, I'd known this since I was a kid (after all, if the unreached could get to heaven some other way, what would be the point of sending missionaries?), but I'd never paused to consider the implications. If you took into consideration all the people who'd ever lived—including those centuries upon centuries when entire continents were cut off from the spread of Christianity—then the vast majority of humanity was going to spend eternity in hell.

I tried to feel out other students to see if anyone else was having similar thoughts, but it was a dangerous subject. Our communal language was so rigid and coded that there was very little vocabulary with which to express doubt. I had to frame my questions as technical doctrinal queries, or else pretend I was seeking evangelism advice ("Say an unbeliever were to ask you to defend the existence of hell . . ."). One evening, in the cafeteria, I suggested that it seemed unfair that people were going to suffer for eternity simply because we believers hadn't managed to bring them the good news. On this point, I got nothing more than a thoughtful nod or a somber "hmm." A few students gave me knowing smiles and little shoulder squeezes, as though I was in the midst of some revelatory spiritual experience that would lead me to the mission field.

On Friday nights, I went down to Michigan Avenue with a dozen other students to do street evangelism. Our team leader was Zeb, a lanky, pimpled Missions major who probably would have been into LARPing or vampirism if he weren't a Christian. Instead, he memorized Luther and Zwingli and made vivid

---

* One day, a student asked about children who died without being saved. Dr. Lightbody gave an answer so tortured and evasive that I had no clue what she was implying until she closed with the caveat "Now, don't ever say that to a mother who's lost a baby." I later found out that Augustine also believed unbaptized infants were sent to hell.

chalk drawings illustrating the plan of salvation, all of which made him kind of popular on campus. We'd set up an easel in front of Banana Republic, and Zeb would draw the abyss that lies between mankind and God, which can be bridged only by the cross, telling the story of redemption as he drew. The rest of us handed out tracts to tourists and businesspeople. We usually drew a small crowd—mostly men who were waiting for their wives to finish shopping and seemed to view us as a zany sideshow. It wasn't one of those vicious "turn or burn" productions, but Zeb's chalk narrative referred to sin and repentance, and the tracts, which had the reasonable title "How to Become a Christian," mentioned hell once or twice. These terms were the water we swam in, but out on the street, against the softly lit backdrop of window displays, they sounded ancient and fierce.

I knew how ridiculous we looked. These people already knew who Jesus was. They'd grown up watching Jerry Falwell spaz out on TV and sneering at Ned Flanders on *The Simpsons*. They didn't know all the theological reasons why God was good, and they would probably never give us the time of day to explain them. We were speaking a foreign language. In a just world, they wouldn't be held accountable for their refusal of the gospel any more than would an unreached person who followed his culture's belief in ancestral worship. When Zeb gave the call to come forward and find forgiveness in Jesus Christ, our audience awkwardly glanced at their watches, put their headphones back on, and moved on.

While I was attending Moody, the most controversial church in the Chicago area was Willow Creek Community Church, out in the northwest suburbs. I'd heard students raving about it—and others railing against it—ever since orientation week. It was

popular among the pastoral, youth ministry, and sports ministry majors. The critics were mostly in the theology department.
Willow Creek's pastor, Bill Hybels, was a well-known author
and something of a celebrity in the evangelical world, but the
big draw was apparently the size of the church. There was a
$73 million "Worship Center," a food court, and a parking lot
worthy of an international airport. Every Sunday morning, a
school bus would pull up to the Moody campus and dozens of
students would climb on board to be bused out to South Bar-
rington for the 9 A.M. service. I had been attending a fledgling
Baptist church in Uptown that year, and when I got back to
the school cafeteria on Sunday afternoons I was routinely confronted with students fresh off the Willow Creek bus, all of
whom were visibly charged, as though they'd just gotten back
from a pep rally. One blustery Sunday morning in February, as
I was walking to the "L" station to catch the train to Uptown,
faced with the prospect of another sixty-five-minute sermon
about gratitude or long-suffering, I found myself suddenly
veering across the campus to get on the Willow Creek bus.

I'd always associated megachurches with televangelists, those
bottle-tanned preachers with southern accents who addressed
the cameras from palatial churches with fountains out front.
Willow Creek was different. The Worship Center seated seven
thousand people, but it was sleek and spare, more convention
hall than cathedral. Hybels preached in a simple Oxford shirt,
and his charisma was muted, reminiscent of the gentle authority assumed by dentists and family physicians. The sermon was
based in scripture. At first, it just seemed like the traditional
gospel set to a brighter tempo. According to Hybels, God's love
was not an unearned gift granted to sinners, but proof that we
mattered on a cosmic scale. Our primary fault was not our sinful nature, but our tendency to think too little of ourselves. We

needed to expand our vision, to stop doubting that we could do amazing things for God. It took me several more visits, over the following few months, before I was able to put my finger on what was off. One Sunday, as I was riding back on the bus, staring out at the mirror-plated corporate headquarters along the freeway, I realized that I couldn't recall anyone at Willow Creek ever mentioning sin, repentance, or confession. I never once heard a reference to hell.

I wasn't aware of it at the time, but Willow Creek was on the front lines of a movement some were already heralding as a "second Reformation," one that had the potential to remake the Christian faith. Hybels was one of a handful of pastors—including, most notably, Rick Warren of Saddleback Valley Community Church in California (author of *The Purpose Driven Life*)—who pioneered what would become known as the "seeker-friendly church," a congregation whose leadership targeted the vast population of Americans who had little to no experience with Christianity ("unchurched Harry and Mary," in ministry lingo). The goal was to figure out why this demographic was turned off by the gospel, and then to create a worship service that responded to their perceived needs.

Essentially, this is consumer-based management.[*] During Willow Creek's inception, Hybels—who studied business before entering the ministry—performed preliminary market research, surveying the unreligious in his community to find out why people weren't going to church. Unsurprisingly, the most common responses were "church is boring," "I don't like being preached down to," and "it makes me feel guilty." Harry and

---

* Hybels keeps a poster in his office that reads: "What is our business? Who is our customer? What does the customer consider value?" Rick Warren's Saddleback motto is "Let the target audience determine the approach."

Mary were made uncomfortable by overt religious symbolism and archaic language. They didn't like being bombarded by welcome committees. The solution was a more positive message: upbeat tunes, an emphasis on love and acceptance. There would be respect for anonymity—visitors wouldn't be required to wear name tags or stand up and introduce themselves. Everything was designed for the visitor's comfort and leisure.

It goes without saying that pastors who are trying to "sell" God won't mention hell any more than a Gap ad will call attention to child labor. Under the new business model, hell became the meatpacking plant, the sweatshop, the behind-the-scenes horror the consumer doesn't want to know about. Once I became aware of what was missing, it was almost a game to watch the ministers try to maneuver around the elephant in the room. One strategy was to place the focus exclusively on heaven, letting people mentally fill in the blank about the alternative. Another was to use contemporary, watered-down translations of the Bible, like *The Message* (reviled around Moody's theology department, where it was better known as "The Mess").

Some Moody students accused Hybels of being a Universalist—a charge lodged against Rick Warren as well, based on his refusal to mention the h-word. But away from the pulpit, these ministers were firmly within the conservative orthodoxy. In his book *Honest to God?* Hybels writes, "I hate thinking about it, teaching about it, and writing about it. But the plain truth is that hell *is* real and real people go there for eternity." Warren admitted essentially the same thing when pressed in an interview: "I believe in a literal hell. Jesus believed in a literal hell. And once you're in, you can't get out." This raises the obvious question: How ethical is it to stand up each week before an audience of people who you believe are going to suffer for all of eternity, and not talk about hell because you "hate thinking about it," or are afraid people will be offended?

At the same time, I realized that Hybels and Warren were responding to the problem we'd noticed down on Michigan Avenue. Most of my friends at Moody disagreed with their approach, but our only other option was to be the ranting voice in the wilderness. It was a hopeless effort, and we all knew it. People looked at our street evangelism team like we were Jesus freaks. (In fact, a number of passersby felt compelled to say as much.) Every Friday night, we'd ride back to campus on the subway in silence, each of us staring slack faced at the crowd of people hooked up to MP3 players and engrossed in fashion magazines. Many of my friends were planning to leave the States after graduation to become missionaries to the developing world. It was not uncommon during those years to hear believers argue that it was far easier to convince people of the existence of hell and the need for salvation in places like Uganda and Cambodia, where the human capacity for evil was not merely an abstraction. Zeb was planning to go to Albania after graduation to plant churches, though he said he worried this was taking the easy way out, like Jonah jumping the boat to Tarsus to avoid bringing the news to the more affluent Nineveh. He said the United States had become so rich and powerful we'd forgotten our need for divine grace.

I started my sophomore year at Moody in September 2001. On the morning of the eleventh, I'd overslept and woke up to my roommate—a soprano in the women's choir—shrieking that we'd been "bombed." There was one television in my dorm, on the second floor, and I made it down there to find the entire female student body crowded around it, watching the footage in silence. An hour later, we were filing into the eeriest chapel service of all time. The overhead lights were off and the television footage was projected onto a large screen at the front of the auditorium. The school president announced that instead of the regular session, we were going to hold a prayer hour, so we split off into circles, holding hands and whispering in the dark, beneath the muted apocalyptic footage. Nobody knew what to say. We were Bible school students—the closest thing to professional pray-ers out there—and yet people stumbled over common phrases and veered into awkward anachronisms like "keep us from evil" and "bestow thy grace." When it was my turn, I squeezed the hand of the girl next to me, signaling for her to go ahead. After the service, they turned the sound back on, but it seemed like the newscasters were just as dumbstruck as we were.

Once the initial shock wore off, you could sense people groping around the cultural junk drawer for appropriate terminology. Newscasters and witnesses referred to Ground Zero as an "inferno" and "hell on Earth." In his address to the nation, George W. Bush said, "Today, our nation saw evil." It was a rhetorical choice designed, as one *New York Times* writer pointed out, "to seek an antique religious aura." Biblical prophecy was revived by conspiracy theorists who tried to prove that the disaster was predicted in the book of Daniel, or who claimed that the architect of the Twin Towers resided at 666 Fifth Avenue. Some witnesses said they glimpsed the mien of Satan in the smoke billowing out of the wreckage. Very quickly, a makeshift theology of good and evil was patched together. The terrorists were "evildoers" who, as Colin Powell put it, were "conducting war against civilized people."

Evangelicals responded with similar vitriol. Billy Graham called the acts "twisted and diabolical schemes," and the Church of the Open Door's David Johnson preached from the book of Revelation, insinuating that the terrorists were a "demonic force in the earth." Around Moody, our professors and administrators kept talking about how the pilots must have been surprised when they woke up expecting to be welcomed by Allah and instead found themselves face-to-face with Jesus and the prospect of eternal suffering. This was said with a belabored sigh that often concealed, I suspected, a note of vindictive satisfaction.

That Sunday, Willow Creek was one of many American churches filled to the brim with newcomers. The Moody bus arrived a little late for the morning service, and we ended up sitting in the uppermost balcony, looking down at the crowd of people seeking spiritual comfort. I was eager to see how Bill Hybels would handle the event—whether he would demonize the enemy or invoke safe platitudes about the brevity of life. As it turned out, he did something completely different. One of the biggest lessons of the past week, he began by saying, was that "evil is alive and well." It was the first time I'd heard the word from his pulpit.

With uncharacteristic gravity, he went on to argue that the evil we'd experienced was not limited to the men who flew the planes. He alluded to the terrorists' accomplices and the people in other countries who were shown celebrating the tragedy. Those actions were evil as well, he said. He spoke of the gas station owners who'd tripled their prices to capitalize on the hysteria and the people who attacked Arab Americans out of rage, at which point the audience hummed in collective disapproval.

The pastor paused for a moment, and then said, "Let's bring it close to home—what about the evil in me? Because boy, I felt it this week." He described the anger he experienced watching the news footage, his immediate craving for revenge. "What is it in us that makes some of us want others to pay a hundred times over for the wrong done to us?" he asked. "Well, that would be evil, and I felt it in me. Did you feel it in you?" With regard to the military response, he argued that Jesus's teaching to not repay evil with evil was just as relevant at a national level. Think about the retaliation that happened all over the world, he said: How was that working out for Sudan? How was it working out for Northern Ireland? The vindictive rage we felt watching the attacks from our kitchen televisions was the same emotion that was creating hell all over the world.

I hadn't felt that rage myself—not because of virtue or self-discipline, but because I was too immature to grasp the full scope of what had happened. It seemed removed and vaguely cinematic. But I did know the feeling he was talking about. It was the same thing I felt when our evangelism team got called Bible-thumpers and Jesus freaks.

I don't know what prompted Hybels to diverge from the market-tested optimism that day, but it was a powerful sermon—people at Moody were talking about it all week. In fact, in a study on the evangelical response to 9/11, this sermon was cited as the only one that questioned the compatibility of military action with Jesus's command to love one's neighbor. The pacifism of the political Left seemed inert and self-flagellating by comparison. Their hesitance to condemn the terrorists, the insistence on the passive voice when describing what had happened, often made it seem as though the attacks had been an act of God, divine punishment for Western imperialism. That Sunday was the only time that someone had asked me to examine myself and my response to the attacks without dismissing their severity or the reality of the human intention behind them. The next Sunday, Hybels preached a message entitled "Religion Gone Awry," about how the backlash against American Muslims ran counter to Christian principles. The following week, he invited Imam Faisal Hammouda to speak at the Sunday service, giving the congregation the opportunity to exercise "discernment" in understanding Islam.

In retrospect, one of the most perplexing things about 9/11 was how swiftly the event congealed and then dissipated from the national consciousness. Half a century ago, when Roosevelt addressed the country after Pearl Harbor, he underscored the severity of the offense by declaring that the nation would not forget it: "Always will we remember the character of the onslaught against us. . . . There is no blinking at the fact that our people, our territory and our interests are in grave danger." Since then, it seems we've come to see prolonged meditation on this kind of horror as a sign of weakness—or perhaps merely a threat to the market. Less than two months after the attacks, Bush noted with pride, "People are going about their daily lives, working and shopping and playing, worshipping at churches and synagogues and mosques, going to movies and to baseball games."

Willow Creek soon got back to business as usual as well, mostly due to the huge backlash against Hybels's decision to "share his pulpit" (as his critics phrased it) with an imam. Apparently the honeymoon was over. People began to find tolerance tedious. Although Hybels didn't apologize for his decision to bring in the imam, he seemed, like any good CEO, to take note of the negative response. In the first sermon of 2002, he encouraged us to put the past year's events behind us and adopt, instead, "an optimistic hope-filled attitude for the year." It was the first message of a sermon series that included titles such as "Wellness," "Family," and "Surviving a Financial Storm." In the end, his radical sermons about collective evil turned out to be aberrational—like many noble acts inspired by the tragedy and then quickly forgotten.

At the time, I didn't appreciate how radical Hybels's 9/11 sermon was. In speaking about his own capacity for revenge and hatred, he had opened up a possibility, a way of talking about evil that was socially and spiritually transformative. It wasn't fire and brimstone; it didn't involve condemning the sinner as some degenerate Other. Rather, he was challenging his congregation to exercise empathy in a way that Jesus might have, suggesting that he among us without sin should cast the first stone.

If I failed to fully consider the possibilities of this theology, it was because I was already in the throes of a spiritual crisis. By the end of that semester, the problem of hell had given way to more serious doubts about Christianity itself, and had so drastically unsettled my faith that I found myself unable to perform the basic rites. When I stood in chapel with my classmates, I was unable to sing along to the hymns in praise of God's goodness; when we bowed our heads to pray, I resorted to pantomime. I left Moody the summer after my sophomore year and took a volunteer position with some missionaries in Ecuador, which was merely an elaborate escape plan—a way to get away from Moody and my parents. Three months into the commitment, I moved to a town in the south of the country where I didn't know anyone, got a job teaching ESL, and stopped going to church entirely.

But people who've gotten that far into the faith never totally shake it. To be a former believer is to perpetually return to the scene of the crime. It's been ten years since I left Moody, and I still find myself stalling on the Christian radio station to hear a call-in debate, or lurking around the religion section of chain bookstores, perusing the titles on the Christianity shelves like a porn addict sneaking a glance at a Victoria's Secret catalog.

In the spring of 2011, I was browsing through an airport newsstand when I glimpsed an issue of *Time* with the headline "What If There's No Hell?" The subhead elaborated, "A popular pastor's bestselling book has stirred fierce debate about sin, salvation and judgment." The book in question was the modestly titled *Love Wins: A Book About Heaven, Hell, and the Fate of Every Person Who Ever Lived*, and the pastor, it turned out, was Rob Bell. Back when I was at Moody, Bell was known primarily as the pastor of Mars Hill Bible Church in Grandville, Michigan—one of the more groundbreaking "seeker churches" in the Midwest. If Hybels was the entrepreneur of the seeker movement, Bell was its rock star. At the time, he favored rectangular glasses and black skinny jeans and looked strikingly like Bono, if you could imagine the laconic machismo replaced with a kind of nerdy alacrity. Most of Bell's congregants were Gen Xers who had difficulty with the Bible's passages about absolute truth, certainty, and judgment. His first book, *Velvet Elvis: Repainting the Christian Faith* (2005), was purportedly aimed at people who are "fascinated with Jesus, but can't do the standard Christian package."

I found a copy of Bell's new book at that same airport and blew through it during my three-hour flight to Michigan. It was a light read. Bell lineates his prose like a free-verse poem, and roughly half the sentences are interrogative, a rhetorical style that seems designed to dampen the incendiary nature of his actual argument. He does not, as the *Time* headline suggests, make a case against the existence of hell. Rather, he argues that hell is a refining process by which all the sins of the world, but not the sinners, are burned away. Those who are in hell are given endless chances throughout eternity to accept God's free gift of salvation and, because this gift is so irresistibly good, hell will eventually be emptied and collapse. Essentially, this is universal reconciliation—the idea that all people will be saved regardless of what they believe or how they conduct themselves on Earth.

Love Wins created an uproar in the evangelical community. Zondervan, a behemoth of Christian publishing that had put out Bell's previous books, dropped him upon reading the proposal, stating that the project didn't fit with their mission. After it was published, Albert Mohler Jr., a prominent reformed pastor, called the book "theologically disastrous," and conservative John Piper tweeted, "Farewell Rob Bell," as if to excommunicate him from the fold. Closer to home, Bell watched as thousands of his congregants left Mars Hill in protest. At the same time, many evangelicals who seemed to have been harboring a private faith in universal reconciliation came out of the woodwork and defended the book. In the secular media, the theology of *Love Wins* was lauded as the radical conception of a visionary. Bell was the subject of a long profile in *The New Yorker*, and *Time* named him one of the most influential people in the world. "Wielding music, videos and a Starbucks sensibility," the magazine wrote, "Bell is at the forefront of a rethinking of Christianity in America."

"Rethinking" is not as accurate as "rebranding." Throughout *Love Wins*, it's obvious that Bell is less interested in theological inquiry than he is in PR. At one point in the book, in order to demonstrate the marketing problems many congregations unwittingly create, he gives a sampling of "statements of faith" from various church websites, all of which depict a traditional Christian understanding of damnation (for example, "The unsaved will be separated forever from God in hell").

Instead of responding to these statements on a theological basis, he remarks, sarcastically, "Welcome to our church." Later on, he reiterates his warning that even the most sophisticated seeker churches won't succeed in attracting unbelievers unless they revamp their theology: "If your God is loving one second and cruel the next, if your God will punish people for all eternity for sins committed in a few short years, no amount of clever marketing or compelling language or good music or great coffee will be able to disguise that one, true, glaring, untenable, unacceptable, awful reality."

Despite Bell's weak hermeneutics, there was one moment when it seemed as though he might initiate a much-needed conversation about the meaning of hell. Toward the end of the book, he begins to mobilize a more radical argument—that heaven and hell are not realms of the afterlife but metaphors for life here on Earth. "Heaven and hell [are] here, now, around us, upon us, within us," he writes. He recalls traveling to Rwanda in the early 2000s and seeing boys whose limbs had been cut off during the genocide. "Do I believe in a literal hell?" he asks. "Of course. Those aren't metaphorical missing arms and legs." For a moment, it seemed as though Bell was going to make a statement as bold and daring as Hybels's 9/11 sermon, using hell as a way to talk about the human capacity for evil.

But soon after he introduces the possibility of a metaphorical hell, he glosses over its significance by suggesting that the "hells" of this Earth are slowly being winnowed away as humans work to remedy social problems like injustice and inequality. He suggests that the Kingdom of God of which Jesus spoke referred not to an eternal paradise, but rather to an earthly golden age (a claim with which few—if any—evangelicals would agree, even if it is commonly accepted among mainline scholars). In his discussion of Revelation, Bell skims over most of the apocalyptic horrors to note that the book ends with a description of "a new city, a new creation, a new world that God makes, right here in the midst of this one. It is a buoyant, hopeful vision of a future in which the nations are healed and there is peace on earth and there are no more tears." Traditionally, evangelicals have interpreted the "new city" as heaven, but Bell's insistence that this new creation is "right here in the midst of this one" defers to a Hegelian understanding of history, one in which humanity improves itself until we've engineered a terrestrial utopia. While this idea is not outside the tradition of Christian eschatology, Bell's version echoes, more than any theological strain, the contemporary gospel of human perfectibility that is routinely hyped in TED talks and preached from the Lucite podiums of tech conferences across the country.

Love Wins succeeded in breaking the silence about hell, and its popularity suggests that a number of evangelicals may be ready to move beyond a literalist notion of damnation, reimagining hell just as God-fearing people across the centuries have done to reckon with the evils of their own age. At the same time, the book demonstrates the potential pitfalls of the church's desire to distance itself too quickly from fire and brimstone. Bell claims to address the exact theological problem that motivated me to leave the faith, but rather than offer a new understanding of the doctrine, he offers up a Disneyesque vision of humanity, one that is wholly incompatible with the language biblical authors use to speak about good and evil. Along with hell, the new evangelical leaders threaten to jettison the very notion of human depravity—a fundamental Christian truth upon which the entire salvation narrative hinges.

Part of what made church such a powerful experience for me as a child and a young adult was that it was the one place where my own faults and failings were recognized and accepted, where people referred to themselves affectionately as "sinners," where it was taken as a given that the person standing in the pews beside you was morally fallible, a fact that did not prevent you from taking her hand in prayer or regarding her as a sister in Christ. This camaraderie came from a collective understanding of evil—a belief that each person harbored within them a potential for sin and deserved, despite it, divine grace. It's this notion of shared fallibility that lent Hybels's 9/11 sermon its power, as he suggested that his own longing for revenge was only a difference of degree—not of kind—from the acts of the terrorists. And it's precisely this acknowledgment of collective guilt that makes it possible for a community to observe the core virtues of the faith: mercy, forgiveness, grace.

The irony is that, at a time when we are in need of potent metaphors to help us make sense of our darkest impulses, Protestant churches have chosen to remain silent on the problem of evil, for fear of becoming obsolete. The short-term advantages of such a strategy are as obvious as its ultimate futility. Like so many formerly oppositional institutions, the church is now becoming a symptom of the culture rather than an antidote to it, giving us one less place to turn for a sober counternarrative to the simplistic story of moral progress that stretches from Silicon Valley to Madison Avenue. Hell may be an elastic concept, as varied as the thousands of malevolencies it has described throughout history, but it remains our most resilient metaphor for the evil both around and within us. True compassion is possible not because we are ignorant that life can be hell, but because we know that it can be.

2014, *The Point*

ON READING UPDIKE

Like so many women who came of age after the turn of the millennium, I was warned about John Updike almost as soon as I became aware of him. There was David Foster Wallace, who, in a 1997 review, popularized the epithet (attributed to a female friend) "Just a penis with a thesaurus." Then there was the writer Emily Gould, who placed him among the "midcentury misogynists"—a pantheon that also included Roth, Mailer, and Bellow. Perhaps most memorably, there was novelist and essayist Anna Shapiro, who claimed that Updike's novels left the female reader "hoping that the men in your own life weren't, secretly, seeing you that way—as a collection of compelling sexual organs the possession of which doomed you to ridicule-worthy tastes and concerns."

Such complaints were pervasive enough by the time I began reading that it was easy for me to dismiss his oeuvre entirely. I would love to concoct some sororal ceremony in which I laid my right hand on *Sexual Politics* and solemnly swore him off, but, in truth, the decision was more incremental, and my reasons more trivial. The criticism I'd read made his writing sound dull. There were too many good books in the world to waste time on a writer whose work was vitiated by ego and roundly despised by writers I admired, and so each time I had the opportunity to read a new author, I chose something else.

In an earlier era, I suppose I would have been made to feel guilty for failing to read an author who is widely considered one of the greatest prose writers of all time. But ignoring him was surprisingly easy. In college, his name had been expurgated from syllabi, replaced with Paula Fox, Joan Didion, and James Baldwin. His true fans, whatever pockets still existed, seemed closeted, hesitant to offer recommendations. Once, in graduate school, I'd griped to a male professor that there were too few novels in the world with believable dialogue. He recommended a few authors, and I dutifully wrote down their names. Then he paused, as though deliberating, and added with a wince, "Also, I hate to say it, but—Updike." It wasn't until later that day, browsing the public library for a copy of *Rabbit, Run* (it was checked out), that I realized it was the same sheepish look assumed by boys at my high school when conceding that Hooters did, actually, have excellent wings.

Earlier this year, I was on vacation in Florida, staying in a low midcentury complex four blocks from the beach. The apartment had terrazzo floors, jalousie windows, and a kitchen outfitted in those matching turquoise appliances manufactured by GE in the 1950s. It was like living in an episode of *Mad Men*. In the backyard, near the pool, stood a laundry hutch filled with used books left by past visitors. It was there, among a shelf crowded with the embossed titles of Dan Brown and

John Grisham, that I discovered a first edition of *Couples*. The dustcover bore a sketch of William Blake's *Adam and Eve Sleeping* washed in turquoise—the same chlorinated blue as the pool and the retro appliances. Maybe it was the tropical air that loosened my defenses and called to mind the promise of that gorgeous prose I'd heard so much about. I decided it was time to give the old letch a shot.

Couples was published in the late '60s, but its story begins in the early years of that decade. Piet, the protagonist, is a thirty-five-year-old building contractor who lives with his family in a fictional Massachusetts town called Tarbox, an old fishing village that has been recently colonized by young Waspy couples who find its decay charming. The narrative point of view often veers away from Piet and travels promiscuously among this circle of couples who spend their plentiful leisure hours playing tennis, hosting dinner parties, and renovating their old saltbox houses. Of this milieu, Updike writes: "They belonged to that segment of their generation of the upper middle class which mildly rebelled against the confinement and discipline whereby wealth maintained its manners during the upheavals of depression and world war." These mild rebellions are not political, but aesthetic.

> Fenced off from their own parents by nursemaids and tutors and "help," they would personally rear large intimate families; they changed diapers with their own hands, did their own housework and home repairs, gardened and shoveled snow with a sense of strengthened health. Chauffeured, as children, in black Packards and Chryslers, they drove second-hand cars in an assortment of candy colors. Exiled early to boarding schools, they resolved to use and improve the local

public schools. Having suffered under their parents'
rigid marriages and formalized evasions, they sought
to substitute an essential fidelity set in a matrix of
easy and open companionship among couples. For the
forms of the country club they substituted informal
membership in a circle of friends and participation in a
cycle of parties and games. . . . Duty and work yielded
as ideals to truth and fun. Virtue was no longer sought
in temple or market place but in the home—one's own
home, and then the homes of one's friends.

The passage immediately called to mind the opening pages
of Jonathan Franzen's *Freedom*, in which a contingent of white
suburban exiles colonizes a not-yet-gentrified city neighborhood in order "to relearn certain life skills that your own parents had fled to the suburbs specifically to unlearn." Perhaps
all bourgeois generations see themselves in similarly pragmatic
terms. Beneath the antiquated details of Updike's description, there are surely echoes of my own generation, whose mild
rebellions have involved learning to make Greek yogurt from
scratch and building tiny houses out of reclaimed wood.

But the residents of Tarbox are also steadfast products of
their time, an era wedged awkwardly between the explosion
of psychoanalysis and the sexual revolution. Whatever subver-
sive pleasure they initially took in shoveling their own drive-
ways and rambling about the garden soon gives way to more
carnal pursuits. Secretive affairs evolve into more transparent
experimentations with spouse-swapping, and soon the matrix
of open marriages becomes so cross-pollinated it's difficult to
keep track of who's swiving whom. The women have begun
going to analysis, the men are hopped up on Freud's 1920 essay
Beyond the Pleasure Principle—and all of the attendant sexual

experimentation has been made possible by the invention of oral contraceptives. The first time Piet cheats on his wife, with her friend Georgene, the mistress replies to his anxious query about birth control with a serene laugh. "Welcome," she says, "to the post-pill paradise."

While the women in the novel are not without sexual agency, there's an obvious power imbalance in all of this experimentation. Even when they initiate affairs, the women are never in control of them; it is the men who dictate the terms and invariably decide when and how they will end. More often than not, women are forced to use sex as a kind of currency—for revenge, for equality—and when they need furtive abortions, they are compelled to trade prurient acts for medical assistance. While the book is not exactly sympathetic to them, the reality of these conditions is rendered with a sharp eye, through characters who are emotionally convincing. For what it's worth, the book does not pretend that swinging—still referred to in those days as "wife-swapping"—benefited all parties in equal measure.

Still, there was plenty in the book that lived up to Updike's contemporary reputation: women who think things no woman would think ("She had wanted to bear Ken a child, to brew his excellence in her warmth"); conversations between women that manage to pass the Bechdel test—in brief: having two women speak to each other about a topic other than a man— only by way of topics related to home renovation; and a panoply of unsettling metaphors ("He fought against her as a raped woman might struggle, to intensify the deed"). There are many passages in which Updike's prodigious gifts as a prose artist are given over to the effects of gravity on women's bodies. Nobody can write the female body in decay quite like Updike. So clinical and unrelenting is his gaze, he manages to call attention to signs of aging that even I—someone in possession of a female body—had never considered. "Age had touched only the softened line of her jaw and her hands," he writes of Piet's wife, Angela, "their stringy backs and reddened fingertips."

The book, when it was published in 1968, landed Updike on the cover of *Time* and sparked a fury of hand-wringing about the country's loosened sexual mores. It appears to have captured that glinting moment in time before swinging became a lifestyle choice and seemed, instead, like a revelation—like something everyone should be doing all the time and from which no ill consequences could be conceived. The novel has often been twinned with Philip Roth's *Portnoy's Complaint*, but its closest analogue is probably the film *Bob & Carol & Ted & Alice*, released the year after *Couples* was published, about a pair of LA couples who decide to experiment with open marriages. Like the thirtysomethings of that film, the residents of Tarbox are too old by the time the country splits apart to join the psychedelic bandwagon, too settled to develop anything like a political imagination. Instead, they use sex as a kind of spiritual salve, a way of keeping their fear of death at bay. "The book is, of course, not about sex as such," Updike said in one interview. "It's about sex as the emergent religion, as the only thing left."

What intrigued me most about *Couples*, though, was the sense of doom that undercuts the orgy. Throughout the book, Piet suffers from nightmares. In one, he dreams he's on a plane that is crashing. He feels the cabin jolt and grips his seat as "the curtains hiding the first-class section billowed." In another, he envisions himself asleep on a frozen pond in the first stages of thaw: "Heavy as lead he lay on the thinnest of ice." Given Updike's abiding thematic preoccupations, it's no great mystery what darkness these dreams portend. "Death stretched endless under him," Piet realizes upon wakening. But the novel is too steeped in the theories of Freud to take the symbolism of such visions literally. Thanatos, after all, is a god with many faces. There is another kind of death, the kind that is synonymous with castration. ("The plane had plunged," he marvels recalling his dream, "and he had been without resources, unchurched, unmanned.") And there is the kind of death that is social, a disruption of the crusty white patriarchal hierarchies that have given rise to this idyll.

Early in the novel, there is a strange moment between Piet and one of his construction operators, "a Negro," whom he chats up one morning at a building site. Piet asks the man whether he's encountered any Indian graves during excavation, and the man admits that he has dug up a few bones here and there. When Piet asks what he does when he encounters them, the operator replies, "Man, I keep movin'," an admission that Piet finds hilarious: "Piet laughed, feeling released, forgiven, touched and hugged by something human arrived from a great distance, imagining behind the casually spoken words a philosophy, a night life." He's taken aback when he realizes the man is not laughing along with him. "The Negro's lips went aloof, as if to say that laughter would no longer serve as a sop to his race."

The moment haunts Piet. He mentions it later to his mistress, referring to it as a "snub," though he "could not specifically locate the cause of his depression, his sense of unconnection." He's equally unhinged by Georgene's insouciance about sex, and recalls her words about the "post-pill paradise" at several moments throughout the novel, like a bellwether of some uncertain future. Tarbox may be paradise, but there is a snake in the garden, and beyond its lush parameters, a storm is gathering.

Indeed, the women of Tarbox become more politically conscious as the story marches through the first half of the decade. Many wives join the Fair Housing Committee; others instigate drunken rows about school integration during the wee, dwindling hours of dinner parties. But Piet, like his male counterparts in town, finds such crusades tiresome. "Politics bored Piet," the narrator notes. His wife drags him along to town meetings, where he passively listens to the townspeople discuss collective agendas, cringing as their eyes "lift in hope toward wholly imagined stars." Piet himself can only feel that celestial ecstasy within the sanctuary of the bedroom. In addition to filling in the lacuna left by religion, sex is supposed to be a surrogate for civic engagement within the moral universe of the novel.

But Piet fails to see the way in which sex itself is becoming political. He has reason to be disturbed by his mistress's welcome into that uncertain paradise. If advanced contraception makes married women more likely to sleep with you, it also means that your own wife (as Piet soon discovers) is more willing to sleep around. It likewise means that women might decide not to marry or have children at all, upending the whole bourgeois religion. The privileged utopia of Tarbox, after all, depends not only on a steady influx of sex, but also on wives who are willing to change diapers with their own hands and cook roast lamb with mint jelly for parties of fourteen.

The year following the debut of *Couples*, Kate Millett published *Sexual Politics*, which called attention to how sexual relations in the novels of D. H. Lawrence, Norman Mailer, and Henry Miller were informed by patriarchic ideals. The '70s would usher in a new wave of feminist critics—in Mailer's words "the ladies with their fierce ideas"—who forever problematized the dominance of that coterie once regarded as the Great Male Novelists. Updike's later books would more consciously wrestle with the specter of his feminist critics, particularly in the satirical parable *The Witches of Eastwick* (a 1984 novel he confessed was written in a spirit of chauvinism) and its more troublesome sequel.

It's hard to imagine that Updike understood, while writing *Couples*, the full bearing that the civil rights movement or the women's movement would have on the culture, not to mention his own legacy. In the end, the novel is not primarily interested in these upheavals, and Updike gave no indication in interviews that the novel's sense of foreboding was meant to symbolize anything other than death. But novels are never unadulterated acts of will—so goes the intentional fallacy. It's arguable, in fact, that the possession of an outsized ego makes a writer even more oblivious to his own vulnerability, making the writing itself more porous to the kinds of anxieties that even Updike himself, with his capacious vocabulary, had difficulty giving a name. *Couples*, like all great novels, can and has been read in myriad ways, but among them it might be regarded as a document of one man's fears about the limits of his own dominion—his dawning premonition that paradise is tenuous, and his to lose.

2016, *The Los Angeles Review of Books*

CONTEMPORARIES

The restaurant is the most popular in town, and we wait the better portion of an hour for a table. There are eight of us gathered on the sidewalk. It's late spring, the kind of mauvish gloaming hour that Virginia Woolf would have marked by the whirling and wheeling of rooks, but there are no rooks here, just dull halos of sodium light and some small brown birds that dart among the shadows, their species unknown to us. We are hungry, and we complain to one another about people who linger at their tables. This is the problem with this town, someone says: there's nothing to do but eat and drink, so everyone camps out at restaurants. Then our reservation is called, and we are led inside, to a private room lit with tallow candles and assembled entirely of old wood.

Most of us present became friends in our late twenties, and some of us are only newly acquainted, but we are the kind of people who speak easily of our internal lives, who regard most social contexts as occasions to divulge the experiences we deem most crucial to our personal development.

One woman, who has recently returned from New Mexico, tells us about the epiphany she had in the wilderness. A year ago, she quit her job and left our town to live in a cabin in the Chihuahuan Desert, where she spent several months meditating "all the time." She appears, as people always do upon returning from places of ample sunshine, brighter and more defined, her silhouette set in stark relief against the backdrop.

One of the men says to her: "When you say you were meditating all the time, what does that mean?"

The woman looks thoughtfully at her empty plate. "I mean it literally," she says. "I don't know how else to describe it. I did guided meditations in the morning and afternoon, and then, when I wasn't sitting, I went out walking and did walking meditation. And I was constantly walking and constantly meditating."

After some time, she tells us, she had a revelation. The revelation was this: she needed to come back here, to the city and the job she had left. She had moved to the desert because she was driven by fear. She had been fine all along. "Then I got sick," she says. "I had a horrible case of the flu. I went around in a daze for a whole week. And then I was better, and all my things were packed into my car, as if by magic."

Some of us have been raised by attentive and encouraging families to speak this way. For others, the skill was learned later in life, in the crucible of identity politics, in defiance of those who would prefer that they remain silent. There are only a few among us—I confess I'm one of them—who are a little embarrassed by the effusions, though in my case the aversion is mostly defensive, a reaction to the self-possession I lack and undoubtedly envy. The truth is I love nothing so much as to hear about the hygiene of other people's souls.

Another woman says, "I've learned that there's a voice in my head that speaks the truth." This woman has recently been diagnosed with cancer. She's nearly a decade older than the rest of us, and whenever she speaks the room becomes very quiet.

"I have lots of voices in my head, but this one is different. It's low, and very calm. And whenever I hear this voice, I stop everything and listen. I heard it a few days after my diagnosis. I was making my bed one morning and worrying, as usual, and the voice in my head said—"

She tells us what the voice said, and we all murmur with approval.

The waiter arrives with the menus. We order mineral water, glasses of red wine, and kombucha that has been crafted in-house. Then: pork confit, fries with truffle oil, and garlic scapes blackened and coiled on a wooden board. I am thinking of the 1969 film *Bob & Carol & Ted & Alice*, which I watched the night before, a movie about the dawn of psychoanalysis in America. In an opening scene, two couples sit in an Italian restaurant and discuss the awakening one pair has had at a spiritual retreat. They speak in reverential tones of the unconscious, repression, breakthroughs. "But how do you feel about that?" they ask one another. Or, if they sense an evasion: "But how do you *really* feel? Be honest." And then they listen to each other, faces pinched with vacant concern, like robots who've just become sentient. Meanwhile, a waiter stands at a cart beside their table, whipping up a pan of zabaglione.

I think: Nothing has changed over the past half century. We are still hopelessly coupling, still confiding to one another at overpriced restaurants our private moments of transcendence. When people look back on our era, they will make no distinction between then and now. It won't matter that we've ceased speaking of Freud, that we've traded zabaglione for lavender macarons. In the future, the whole swath of late modernity will call to mind the image of people eating delicacies and talking about the state of their souls—just as, when someone mentions the medieval period, we picture people toiling in ditches.

When I was young, I often imagined that my life was being observed by people from the past. It was one of those voyeuristic games children invent to relieve the essential tedium of childhood, to lend consequence to an overabundance of time. Riding my bike along the streets of our town, I would try to picture everything that entered my field of vision as it might be perceived by people from the time of Moses, or of Plato. That my spectators were always people from the past meant, I suppose, that I believed I was living in the future. In fact, the pleasure of the game derived from imagining that these historic people were seeing, for the first time, a drawbridge, a digital marquee, a yellow Corvette. It was a way to see these things myself. I was told, of course, that God was watching, but the problem with God was omniscience. A lens that captures everything is no longer a lens. What I craved was another subjective consciousness, a point of reference that could reveal something about my place in time.

Several years ago, around the time I turned thirty, my doctor sent me to the big university hospital for an MRI. We already knew that the lump in my head was a tumor, but the scan would determine how big it was and whether it could be extracted through surgery. As I lay there with my head in the tunnel of the scanner, I found myself reverting to my childhood game. I considered the machine, how strange it was. It occupied an entire room. The voice of a woman I'd never met instructed me, through a speaker near my ear, how to position my head. I thought: I am a person of the future, enclosed in this synthetic cocoon that uses particle physics to capture the insides of bodies. But then, in almost the same moment, the technology seemed to me barbaric. The machine was loud and clunky and used radiation. It was made by the same electronics company that manufactured my mother's overheating dishwasher. The cab driver who had taken me to the hospital claimed it could give you cancer. Throughout the rest of the session, these two images—the machine as futuristic wonder, the machine as primitive contraption—existed simultaneously in my mind, like a hologram.

Ever since then, I think only of how our lives will be viewed retrospectively by our descendants. The tenor of my game has become tragic, and its visions arrive automatically now, without my choosing them. It tends to happen when I am most happy, surrounded by friends and good food and gentle light, and I cannot stop the thought from entering my mind: "How happy we were," as though I am witnessing an idyll that will be obliterated by a coming horror. But the horror never comes. Instead, the ease of our lives is interrupted by isolated acts of violence that eat up the news cycle and disrupt our sleep and begin, over time, to seem unrelated.

Most of the people I know are obsessed with the present. They would correct my phrasing, though: It's not about history, but a mental state. Being present. Becoming present. They spend hours each week practicing breathing techniques and contorting their bodies into unnatural postures in order to focus without distraction on that which lies directly in front of their noses. The idea, as I understand it, is to dilate the mind's eye for maximum sensory intake. If you can reduce the mechanisms of your psyche to a glacial speed, placing four walls around this very moment, you'll be able to capture it all: the color of the grass and all its shades and variations; not only the flavor of the food, but its undertones and subtle pockets of brightness. Of course, the obstacles to this state of mind are multitude: children, lunch dates, anxiety, to-do lists. But most of all it is the devices. It is the devices, especially, I'm told—the pods and the pads and the wristbands and watches—that have colluded to whisk us away from the Eternal Now.

When I try to envision the Eternal Now, I picture a room without windows or doors, like a stage production of *No Exit*. It is a room that exists nowhere in particular. In lieu of context, in lieu of vista, one is forced to find meaning in the microscopic details of the room itself, which must inevitably come to seem intricate and endless: the cracks in the wall, the wood grain that striates the floorboards. A universe in miniature. It's difficult for me to see how this state of mind constitutes a retreat from the logic of the internet—that lens that captures everything. To exist within that room of perpetual updates and endless opinions is to believe that history can be divided not by centuries but by seconds, that every idea must lead to finer sub-points and infinite distinctions that ultimately contradict one another. I sometimes wonder whose job it will be to weed through our digital garbage and make sense of it all. Graduate students, I suppose—if there are graduate students in the future. And they will be forced to conclude that everything that could possibly be said about us was true, as well as its opposite: that our souls were vitiated by decadence; that we were creatures of self-denial; that we indulged the flesh; that we were not vigilant about self-care; that we had become barbaric; that we had become effete; that we consumed too much fat; that we did not consume enough.

Perhaps the essential appeal of the digital world is its capacity not to distract us from the present but to clench us in its maw. There is something hypnotic in its assurance that nothing lies beyond the day's serving of novel minutiae. To leave this world, even for an hour, is to find yourself drifting uncertainly beyond the margins of the moment. Your mind begins to wander, or else you find yourself slipping uneasily into the past. A few weeks ago, a friend of mine arrived at the gym and discovered that he'd forgotten both his phone and his headphones at home.

"What did you do?" I said.

"I spent an hour on the elliptical thinking about my regrets." He smiled sadly, the way people my age have only begun to—a tentative wistfulness. "That day," he said, "I got a *real* workout."

Although it would have seemed absurd only a short time ago, it is now possible to conceive of eating at restaurants as an act of courage, just as it has become plausible to view any number of ordinary pleasures—doing lakefront yoga, sampling truffles, reading *The New York Times*—as fragile and therefore historically meaningful. It is possible to think this way (indeed, hardly anyone discourages it) because there are people who want to stop us from doing these things; who impart violence to keep us from dancing in clubs and going to concerts and eating delicacies while discussing the state of our souls. Nobody mentions these people that night at the restaurant, as the eight of us sit in the candlelit room made entirely of wood, but the most recent attack is still fresh enough that its presence is felt nonetheless. The danger itself is not real to us, but there is a certain energy in the room, an unspoken conviction that we are part of a common enterprise; that the idle and forgettable tasks that previously occupied our days are now undertaken deliberately, in a spirit of defiance. This is another way of seeing.

The sky outside the window turns from pink to blue to black, and once the food is cleared away, our conversation grows sober. We confess that we're forgetting things we used to know; that technology is developing faster than we can assimilate ourselves to its alterations; that growing older feels, in many ways, like backpedaling. We are trying to convey that time for us has ceased to feel real. We cannot conceive of the next dispensation. The only people who have a clear vision of the future, it occurs to me that evening, are those enemies of liberalism. But their vision is insane.

I say: "I wonder if it's different for people who have kids." All of us present are childless. I try to explain that when a person has a child, they feel invested in the progression of history. I'm thinking of my sisters, how they've become, through motherhood, less cynical about the future. I'm thinking, too, about the end of *The House of Mirth*, when Lily Bart holds the servant woman's baby and feels, for the first time in her life, anchored in time. "All the men and women she knew were like atoms whirling away from each other in some wild centrifugal dance: her first glimpse of the continuity of life had come to her that evening in Nettie Struther's kitchen."

The woman who has recently returned from New Mexico interrupts me. "But people with children never think about these things. They're too busy—or else they see it as frivolous."

Everyone agrees: We hear things of this sort all the time from our friends who have children. "I used to think about existential questions, but now the only thing in my head is diapers and feeding times." This is, in fact, the draw of having children, says a woman sitting across from me: the ability to drown out all philosophical concerns with the exigencies of maintaining another person's life; to batten down the progression of time with an ongoing state of emergency.

But of course we are too self-aware, the eight of us, to let such a statement stand. Someone points out that we ourselves are no better. All of us have our distractions, our self-delusions, our ways of avoiding the dull baseline of reality.

One of the writers remarks that the best advice he ever got about character development was to ask oneself: What is the lie this character harbors about himself? "All of us have a lie that we hinge our entire lives on," he says.

"That's horrible," one woman replies, "to think of what it might be."

There is a long moment of silence, and then the woman who has been diagnosed with cancer speaks. "You probably know what it is, though," she says to the other woman. Then she gestures broadly, including the entire table. "All of us probably know, implicitly, what our lie is. Just think about it."

The room again grows silent, and for a moment there's a vital, almost giddy energy among us. Everyone seems to be simultaneously looking, and trying very hard not to look, at the person across from them. Then the waiter comes to drop off the check. We look at the time. Outside, there is still a line of customers waiting on the sidewalk to be seated. It's late, we conclude; we should go. One man lays down a credit card, and the rest of us send him money invisibly, through our phones.

"We hated those people who were lingering at their table," I say, as we stand to leave. "And now we are those people."

Someone else says: "It's the circle of life."

———

For a long time afterward, I recalled the moment at the restaurant when we all looked at one another across the table, each of us ostensibly thinking about our lie. What was clear in that moment was that we all believed we could correctly identify our own self-deception, a conviction that seemed, the more I considered it, peculiar to people my age. Unlike the disciples of Freud, who sought to lay naked the hard knob of truth at the core of their existence, we are content merely to insist that we're cognizant of the delusions that animate our lives, that we can approximate their location in the byways of our psyches. ("Don't *do* anything," the facilitator said the one time I tried meditating, when I inquired what to do about runaway thoughts. "Just be aware of them.") But the more I thought about this assumption, the more I came to find its premise absurd.

Throughout my twenties, I was a prolific journaler. I filled pages of Mead notebooks with self-analysis and self-diagnosis. I still have these notebooks, and when I go back and read them today, I am struck by two things: one, how relentlessly self-aware I was. In each entry, I dissect my own faults and delusions with unflinching vigilance, circling back to each statement to offer caveats and addendums. "I realize, of course," begin so many transitions. Or once: "Don't for a second think I'm unaware. . . ." And yet the second thing that strikes me is how, despite these interrogations, I remained patently unaware of the most obvious truths about myself. Things that would be clear to any sane reader are circled and evaded with an ignorance that is almost farcical. It is as though I was capable of seeing everything except that which was most obvious, except the thing that was right in front of me.

Awareness is not the same as perspective; sometimes the former is an obstacle to the latter.

A man I used to know, a pastor, once said that self-awareness was the consequence of original sin, that first error committed in the primordial garden. Humans were once as happy as lambs, munching the grass, unaware of their minds or their bodies. It was greed that set us apart from the animals. We desired a knowledge of ourselves that was meant for God alone and could not but doom us to unhappiness. This, of course, is the Christian view of things: that we were better off as sheep.

Now we are passing this curse on to the inanimate things of this world. I live in a house full of objects that are slowly becoming conscious: a thermostat, a coffeemaker, a computer, a phone. Throughout the day, they watch me and blink their blue lights and silently gather information, and on some days I believe, along with the optimists, that they will soon tell us everything we care to know about ourselves. But I do not sleep well. My dreams are rife with shadows and menace, and the house, during those hushed hours before dawn, seems to groan beneath the weight of those budding brains. Increasingly there are nights when I sit up in bed, awakened by the panic of some half-remembered thought, one of those foundational problems that gets lost in the wash of secondary concerns and emerges only when you are loose and unguarded to remind you, with a start, that you've forgotten the original question; that you're missing the point.

2017, *Ploughshares*

A SPECIES OF ORIGINS

The dinosaur billboards start appearing around Chicago: THE BLAZING BRACHIOSAURUS, THE SWIFT PTERODACTYL. We see them throughout Illinois, Indiana, Michigan, and Ohio. The illustrations are vintage comic book: colorful, muscular animals bursting out of the confines of the frame. Sauropod necks stretch down toward the street. A triceratops bolts headlong into the blue, ready to pounce on an oncoming car. Their names are stamped in block text, bold and bright and selectively alliterative. THE MIGHTY MASTODON, THE SUPER RAPTOR.

"Why not the Rapacious Raptor?" asks my boyfriend, Barrett, who is along for the ride. "Or the Rapturous Raptor?" It's ninety-eight degrees outside, and we're driving down the freeway with the windows down because my car's AC is broken. Both of us are starting to get a bit batty from the heat.

"Or the Raptured Raptor," I say.

"Raptured?" he shouts over the wind.

"Taken by God. Raptured."

He absently tugs at his beard and says, after a moment, "So that's what happened to the dinosaurs."

Imagine the Ark in all its glory: an ancient ship, built of pine, fir, and cedar, rising out of the hills of Northern Kentucky. It will be taller than the Giza pyramids, longer than an American football field by a good one hundred feet, and shaped like a cargo ship, with a cambered roof and a small stern projection like a rudder. On board, there will be animals: zebras and monkeys, alligators and ostriches. The robotic beasts will appear incredibly lifelike, with roving eyes and real fur and iridescent scales of molded foam rubber. The ship will sit on eight hundred acres of bluegrass near I-75, the busiest North-South interstate in the nation, but it won't be visible from the highway. This is intentional. Ken Ham, the Australian visionary behind the Creation Museum, claims that the whole point of the Ark Encounter is for people to *encounter* it (as the name suggests)—to have an experience with the historic truth it represents. This can't happen if commuters are just gawking at the ship from their cars during rush-hour gridlock. The Ark is a boat that can change lives, a boat that has the power to prove God's Word is the truth. It's also a $73 million project, slated to open in 2016, with construction beginning this year. (The attraction officially opened in July 2016.)

I'll be the first to acknowledge there are few things more odious than the marriage of evangelism and big-budget productions. But when I first heard about the Ark Encounter while surfing around the Christian blogosphere (as we former believers are apt to do), some atavistic part of me was fascinated with the project. Throughout my childhood, I'd regarded Ken Ham as a bona fide celebrity. Back in the '90s, long before the Creation Museum came into being, my homeschool group would get together to watch videos of his seminars for the Institute for Creation Research: lectures about how the dinosaurs became extinct (humans killed them) or why the platypus sinks the whole theory of evolution. This was when he was in his early forties, sporting overgrown Abe Lincoln chops that made his face seem remarkably (and unfortunately) simian. He managed to strike us kids as a trustworthy enough source, delivering factoids in his cool Aussie accent. He was an avuncular science guru—the fundamentalist response to Bill Nye, minus the bow tie and the zany fun. Incidentally, Ham faced off against Nye earlier this year, in a webcast debate about the merits of creation science. Many commentators noted that the debate was over long before it started, citing Nye's willingness to engage with creationism as a legitimate scientific position. As one writer noted in *The Daily Beast*, "Ham won this debate months ago, when Nye agreed to participate."

My siblings and I were, in many ways, your typical young-Earth creationist kids. Our parents homeschooled us so that we wouldn't be exposed to things like evolutionary biology, and they took us to summer camps where we were taught how to debate "secular science." I wasn't allowed to see *The Land Before Time* because it alluded to the Earth being billions of years old. By eight, I had memorized ocean salinity stats to persuade unsaved kids that the Earth couldn't possibly be more than six thousand years old. By twelve, I knew to raise my hand whenever someone mentioned "millions of years" and say, "Excuse me, sir/madam: Were you there?"

Noah's ark is the story most frequently ridiculed by opponents of biblical literalism, and the Ark Encounter is designed to demonstrate that it was indeed possible for a ship of this size to hold two of every kind of animal living today, plus those that are now extinct, like the dodo and the quagga—not to mention the Blazing Brachiosaurus, the Mighty Mastodon, and the Super Raptor.

My parents, who've visited the Creation Museum many times since it opened in 2007, have been urging me to visit the museum for years, suggesting that I might find it "interesting" (read: conversion inspiring). And my Facebook feed is perennially littered with posts from my old Moody Bible Institute friends claiming the museum is "powerful" and "faith affirming." But it wasn't until the Creation Museum announced it would be holding an information session on the Ark Encounter and that Ken Ham would be there in the flesh, accompanied by the Ark design team, that I finally got up the courage to head south for a few days and see what all the fuss was about.

The museum is less than a mile off the exit, on an otherwise empty country road. It's a low, militant-looking building with the smoke-tinted windows of a corporate office park. Security guards in aviators and khaki uniforms stand outside each of the entrances.

"I thought this place was supposed to be huge," Barrett says.

"Maybe there are more buildings," I say, gathering my things.

"What kind of museum has armed security outside?"

"They're not armed."

"He's got a gun on his hip."

"It's probably a Taser."

"He's got a Taser and a gun. Look."

It's Saturday morning, and I have Barrett drop me off at the back of the parking lot, mostly because I need a few minutes to mentally prepare myself for the museum. Already there are the bumper stickers (EVEN JESUS HAD A FISH STORY), and the church buses, and the fifteen-passenger converted cargo vans favored by families with more than six children (my folks had one throughout my teen years). Already, there are kids in those T-shirts—the ones emblazoned with familiar logos that, upon closer inspection, turn out to be evangelical knockoffs. (*The Hunger Games* is actually HUNGER FOR GOD. One girl's shirt has the Apple logo, but the caption reads iTRUST.)

Legacy Hall, the museum's main auditorium, is a sleek windowless room that seats about a thousand. On this day it's not quite at capacity, but it seems overflowing with humanity. All around me, there are men with fresh crew cuts, women with self-tinting prescription glasses, and teenagers so behind mainstream fashion they could be mistaken for hipsters in their high-waisted jeans and Ukrainian crown braids. When Ken walks up to the podium, there's no applause or cheering, but the sound of conversations dissolves to whispers. After welcoming the crowd, he says he wants to begin with something that's kind of difficult to say. It's difficult to say because America has been the greatest Christian nation on Earth. We have the largest number of churches, Bible colleges, seminaries, and Christian bookshops in the world. "But it's true that when you look at the structure in America," he says, "it's becoming less and less Christian every day. We've entered an era of cultural relativism."

The first part of his talk is a ballistic CliffsNotes version of a speech I've heard pastors give hundreds of times, the gist of which is that the advent of postmodernism in America has destroyed the authority of God's Word. Ken's special take on this dilemma is that relativism has gone so far as to infiltrate Christianity itself: just as the secular world has taken liberties with absolute truth, so the church has found creative loopholes within scripture, in order to believe whatever they want to believe.

Ken looks down and shifts through his notes. "People say to me, 'Ken, why Noah's ark?' Well, the ark continues to capture the imagination of the general public. In fact, the Flood is one of the few historical events that is well known in almost all cultures and religions." (Much of the Ark Encounter's publicity materials contain similar references to the "worldwide flood myth." It's the kind of strategic faux pluralism commonly used by evangelical organizations in public discourse.) The Ark also happens to be the perfect tool for evangelism. In addition to the story being a literal event that took place here on Earth, Ken says, the Flood was also intended to be a metaphor about salvation. I vaguely recall this interpretation from my Bible college days: John 10 refers to Christ as "the gate" through which we pass to salvation. Noah and his family were saved by walking through the door of the ark. We too can be saved through faith in Jesus Christ.

Ken shows some video clips that use sweeping CGI shots to give us a better sense of the scope of the ark, then puts up a colorful illustration of the entire park, which looks like nothing so much as a page from *Where's Waldo?*—the cartoonish Boschian chaos. The Ark is merely the first stage of the project. Plans have already been made to phase in future attractions, event venues, theaters. There will be a parade of live animals outside the Ark, where an actor playing Noah will lead the menagerie on board while his pagan neighbors heckle and ridicule him. There will also be a Tower of Babel, a Ten Plagues ride, and a re-created Noah's village that will include "live pagan entertainment."

Ken introduces the Ark design team: Pat Marsh, the art director, used to work for Universal Studios, where he designed the Jaws and King Kong attractions. The head illustrator Jon Taylor did projects for Mattel, Fisher-Price, and Milton Bradley. For the most part, this is the same design team that helped develop the Creation Museum. As a way of praising his designers, Ken notes that a number of secular visitors have been disturbed by the quality of the museum. "One of them went home and wrote an article," he says. "And he said in that article, 'That place is dangerous. It's so well done; kids are going to believe it!'"

The auditorium erupts in applause, hooting and hollering more emphatically than they have all morning. I glance around the theater to see if anyone else is baffled by this response. According to Ken's anecdote, the visitor was making an observation about the design quality—a specious sleekness that might succeed in fooling a child. But judging by the tenor of the cheers (the exasperated eye rolls, the muttered *Can you just believe that?*), the crowd is applauding the triumph of creation science itself. It's as if everyone is tacitly agreeing that there's no distinction between truth and the quality of its presentation.

The Lord's Day vibe at the Creation Museum is remarkably different from the Saturday crowds. When I come back on Sunday, the place is near-empty. Noah's Café and the ice cream stand closed early in the afternoon, and there are fluffy harp hymns piped into the exhibits, like an apology for the silence. The museum workers are visibly relaxed, joking with one another and eager to talk to guests. And Barrett, bursting with confidence, poster child of the American public schooling system, is wandering up to complete strangers and starting conversations. Every time I leave his side—to go to the restroom, or wander off to the next exhibit—I come back to find him chatting up the staffers. We meet Joyce and Greg, a fifty-something couple wearing the museum uniform of khaki excavator vests and safari hats. They're originally from Portland, Oregon, but moved out to Kentucky just "to be a part of all this," including the upcoming Ark Encounter. Years ago, they worked for the Holy Land Experience in Orlando ("before it got bought out by Trinity Broadcasting Network," Joyce is careful to add) and did some work with Campus Crusade. "We think Ken is just great," Joyce says. "He's like a modern-day Josiah, getting people back into the Word."

One of the central exhibits of the museum is a series of tableaux about the origins of the world. The much-hyped Garden of Eden turns out to be an explosion of fake greenery that, like most biblical utopias (heaven, the promised land, the millennial Earth), seems suffocating in its unmitigated perfection. The animatronic Adam and Eve are swarmed with friendly animals, while a T. rex looms in the corner, chomping on leaves (since there was no death in the pre-Fall world, it goes without saying that all animals were originally herbivores). Barrett wants to know why, if Adam and Eve were not ashamed of their nakedness, the mannequins' private parts are strategically covered by apple blossoms, and I have to explain that even though the silicone Adam and Eve are sexual innocents, the museum patrons are regular old fallen humans who might be more than a little aroused by extremely lifelike nude animatronics. The exhibits are somewhere in the ballpark of Disney-caliber but betray a campy self-awareness (there are exhibit signs that read, THOU SHALT NOT TOUCH, PLEASE!).

According to the exhibit, the Fall ushered in not only death and suffering, but such specific phenomena as genetic mutations, excessive cell reproduction rates (leading to cancer), and parasitism. Once sin entered the world, animals began overproducing in order to replace the ones killed off by diseases and predators, and, as a result of this, even horticulture changed. In the Garden of Eden, plants produced only the amount of food necessitated by animal diets. However, after the Fall, when animals proliferated, God introduced overproduction of plants, resulting in weeds. In fact—this is something I hadn't heard before—even human intelligence was tainted, over time, by the Fall. Adam and his descendants had a brain capacity that surpassed that of any human living today. This explains how Noah was able to use shipbuilding technology that wasn't around until centuries after the Flood.

As I browse the exhibits, it becomes clear that in the decades since I was a kid, creationists have evolved into a more sophisticated species, particularly in their efforts to reconcile scripture with empirical, observable evidence. Their methods are far from scientific, but there's a willingness to compete with legitimate science that wasn't present in the past. It's not so much anti-intellectualism as it is intellectualism conceived on another planet, by scientists stoned on hallucinogens, watching reruns of Carl Sagan's *Cosmos*. Creationists now have their own research institutes and their own peer-reviewed journals that feature articles like "Emergentism and the Rejection of Spirit Entities: A Response to Christian Physicalists."

As someone who grew up immersed in creationism, I never thought about whether it was an attractive worldview—it was simply the Truth. Ironically, it was only after I stopped believing in God—for unrelated reasons—that I began to regard creationism as a deeply seductive belief system. After I left the faith, I read Richard Feynman and Stephen Jay Gould, and as I confronted the specter of a universe determined by phenomena as bizarre as virtual particles and Boltzmann brains, I often felt a pang of nostalgia for the elegance of the Genesis narrative. The truth is that even when it's dressed up in pseudoscientific jargon, creationism's appeal lies in its delicious simplicity. It presents the kind of tidy framework physicists dream about: a unified theory of everything—and one that hasn't been revised in six thousand years. By the time I got around to the books of Brian Greene, by contrast, people were already debating whether string theory had been debunked by the Large Hadron Collider.

Real science is mind-bogglingly complex and beginning to sound more and more like science fiction (multiverses, spiritual machines). The pressing questions about the origins of the universe have moved from the realm of biology (user-friendly, fun) to that of physics (arcane, counterintuitive), and this shift is coinciding—at least in this country—with shortening attention spans, at a time when truth often gets confused with the most pithy sound-bite. Creationism, which (like many forms of alternative facts) relies on oversimplified, passionate appeals to common sense, might actually have an adaptive edge in this climate.

One of the museum's most recent additions, the Lucy exhibit, is designed to provide a creationist perspective on the famous bipedal hominid unearthed in 1974—one of the most definitive pieces of evidence that humans descended from apes. Up on the wall, there's a large plaque with the title START-ING POINTS SHAPE OUR INTERPRETATION OF THE EVIDENCE. On the other side of the room, under a glass box, there is a reconstructed skin-and-hair model of the creationist version of Lucy. Instead of standing upright, as she's normally shown, the model is hunched in the classic knuckle-dragging pose and covered in hair. When you step to the side of the box, ghostly blue holographic bones appear beneath her skin, showing how the skeleton that was discovered was incomplete. The point is that researchers use significant "artistic license" to put flesh to the bones of their discoveries.

I turn back to the exhibit hall to look for Barrett and find him cornered by a tall gangly man in a green T-shirt. The two of them are standing beneath the STARTING POINTS plaque.

"So you're operating from the premise that Christianity is a bias," Barrett says, gesturing to the text above them.

"I don't admit that it's a bias," the man says. "I said that it's a starting point. Those are two very different things." He's wearing a crew-neck shirt bearing the ill-advised Bob Jones University acronym: BJU. He has deeply bronzed skin and a smile that looks catalog bought. I hang back, pretending to look at the Lucy model, hoping to eavesdrop on their conversation.

"Well, what's your definition of a starting point?" Barrett asks.

"Listen," the guy says, in a low, but measured tone. "You and I, we both have the same evidence. We live on the same Earth, correct?"

Barrett seems to pause for a split second, then says, "OK."

"But how we interpret that evidence differs based on our worldview."

"That's relativism."

The man gives out a low laugh. "No, sir. That is not relativism."

"If truth is dependent on—"

"Listen, listen, listen. You're confusing my argument."

"I don't think I'm confusing it at all. The Bible is one starting point. Darwin is another."

At that moment, something happens that isn't, I suppose, all that surprising. I forget which side I'm on. "The Bible is from the Creator, though," I say.

The man turns around and barely registers my presence before pointing at me. "Bingo."

Barrett looks at me like I've just shown him a heretofore concealed swastika tattoo.

"He's not saying there are no absolutes," I tell him. "He's just saying that your interpretation of physical evidence is going to be incorrect if you don't accept the Bible as the truth."

"So your starting point is the Truth," Barrett says, looking slowly from me to the man, then back again. "You've already decided what reality is."

"We didn't decide," the man says. "God decided. He's the Creator. He was there, in the beginning. Were you there in the beginning of the world?"

"No," Barrett says. He keeps looking at me with the deflated gaze of the betrayed. I turn toward the next exhibit, hoping he'll follow me, but instead he launches into what I can already tell is a doomed line of argument: questioning the veracity of scripture itself. He points out that the Genesis story was based on Egyptian creation myths.

The man winces. "Come on, now. You honestly believe that?"

"It's not what I believe," Barrett says. "It's the truth. Read any historian—"

"Any *secular* historian."

"These are people who've devoted their lives to studying primary sources and publish their results in peer-reviewed journals—"

"I have my sources too."

"—and have advanced degrees and work for research foundations that—"

"So do my sources."

"—are known around the world. . . . ."

The man smiles at me with a kind of long-suffering good humor, as if we're the only two reasonable people in this conversation. He squeezes Barrett's shoulder and I realize suddenly in this gesture, in its assured familiarity, that he's a pastor. He glances at me as he turns to leave. "Try and talk some sense into this guy, will you?"

After picking at a Fossil Cake (the museum's version of funnel cake), Barrett and I find ourselves veering into the lobby theater to see a showing of *Global Warming: A Scientific and Biblical Exposé of Climate Change*. It appears to be a pretty traditional science documentary, like something that might have been shown on the Discovery Channel circa 1995 (before the slogan changed from "Explore Your World" to "Entertain Your Brain"). Interviews with scientists are spliced with pedestrian footage of flowers blooming, waves crashing on amber sand. The scientists are, at first glance, more credible than I expected them to be. Most have a "Dr." in front of their name and belong to institutions that, while obscure, sound like more than mere degree mills. One of them, Dr. Roy Spencer, is a former NASA climatologist who claims, "There isn't anybody I know today that doesn't agree that we are unusually warm right now." Just as I'm beginning to wonder if perhaps the filmmakers mis-understood the word "exposé," the shot of Dr. Spencer stalls in a freeze-frame, and the narrator's ominous voice says, "But that's where the agreement amongst scientists ends."

"That's right," whispers one of the women in front of us. Barrett and I are seated behind a row of about a dozen fifty-something women clutching Vera Bradley bags. These women are incredibly vocal throughout the film, offering Pentecostal-like affirmations after every sound-bite.

The scientists argue that the current warmth has nothing to do with human culpability and take turns providing alternate theories: sunspots, changes in the ocean circulation, and fluctuations in our wind systems might all be culprits for the warmth. "There's something going on with sunlight that we don't understand," says Dr. Spencer.

Many of the scientists take jabs at *An Inconvenient Truth* (one refers to it as "Al Gore's crockumentary," which receives a glee-ful round of applause from the Amen Corner) for its "doomsday scenarios" and its use of "dramatic footage" of glaciers melting and rising sea levels. Climate change, in other words, is mere media hype—a sensational narrative that news networks play up in order to keep eyeballs locked on their product.

Then the video takes an unexpected turn. There's footage of Cambodia, South Africa, Albania—canvas tents and dung fires and ectomorphic children with bloated bellies. The narra-tor informs us that one million Africans die each year because of lack of access to electricity. The reason? Western environ-mentalists have convinced their governments to prevent the construction of hydroelectric dams. "We're sacrificing the poor at the altar of radical environmentalism," says one of the sci-entists. The film ends with God's promise to Noah in Genesis 8:22: "While the Earth remains, seedtime and harvest, cold and heat, and summer and winter, day and night, shall not cease."

As the theater lights come on and people begin filing out of their rows, Barrett and I just sit there, blinking away the brightness, listening to the dwindling voices of the other patrons.

While the Earth remains.

As we sit in the emptying theater, I realize what was missing from the film—not the beginning, but the end. After all, believers know that a worldwide catastrophe is, without a doubt, coming. It's not preached much from the pulpit these days, but my Christian friends and family members often remind me that God will return to destroy the world. The Gospel of Matthew says, "As it was in the days of Noah, so it will be at the coming of the Son of Man." Of course, many evangelicals believe that by the time the apocalypse hits, the followers of Jesus will have been raptured, taken away to heaven. Like Noah and his family, they will be plucked out of the chaos and allowed to watch from a safe distance as God destroys the Earth: the plants and animals, the mountains and the seas, the rivers and the deserts. All of it consumed by fire. If this is how the world ends—if God has such little regard for his own creation—then why should his followers bother trying to preserve it? The irony is that Ken is building an ark—a symbol of global catastrophe—at a moment when our seawaters are rising and environmental disasters of a biblical scale are becoming a real possibility.

Outside the Creation Museum, dark rafts of cumulus clouds are amassing, threatening a storm. We get in the car, driving away along a stretch of parched farmland, the fields gone sallow from the recent drought. Barrett flips through some of the museum's promotional brochures before tossing the glossy pamphlets into the backseat. "I don't understand why Ken is even bothering to build the Ark. Why does he need to spend all this money and waste all these resources to prove something he already knows is true?"

"It's not for him," I say. "He's making it for people like us. So we'll come here skeptical and be converted by the truth."

"You think that'll happen?"

"To me?"

"To anyone."

I'd like to say no, but I'm not so sure. Ken is fond of ranting against the evils of postmodern relativism, where opinion carries more weight than fact, and all evidence is subject to interpretation. Yet this is precisely the environment that allows pre-Enlightenment thinking like creationism to thrive. If Ken Ham's worldview is considered a viable product in the marketplace of ideas, it's because ours is a culture that has lost faith in objective authority—one where opinions are swayed not by the integrity of the argument but by the pyrotechnics of its presentation.

When I was a kid, the church saw itself in opposition to this sort of relativism—an island amid a sea of shifting truths. And I suppose that in coming to the Creation Museum, the backwater fringe of evangelicalism, I'd expected to find some remnant of this older, near-extinct form of Christianity—one unconcerned with passing fashions, one that was secure in the mysteries of scripture. Instead, I found the church's latest attempt to bewitch unbelievers with glitzy multimillion-dollar productions. Evangelicals like to claim that theirs is a religion of immutable absolutes, and yet attractions like the Ark Encounter belie the church's increasing willingness to engage in the kind of market-driven natural selection that increasingly determines "truth" in our culture—call it the survival of the slickest. It's a worldview that precludes the very possibility of inconvenient truths.

As we head north, I roll down the windows. The sky has gone black, and the air possesses the damp coolness of the hours that precede a storm. But as we continue our drive home, the sky clears, and night falls, and days pass before the rain finally comes.

2014, Oxford American

THE INSANE IDEA

Last April, the *Atlantic* published a feature-length takedown of America's longest-standing mutual aid fellowship. "The False Gospel of Alcoholics Anonymous" was the work of Gabrielle Glaser, who delivered the bad news in dry and dismal statistics. According to modern studies, AA's success rate is between 5 and 8 percent. Glaser claimed she was surprised by the numbers ("I assumed as a journalist that AA worked"), though the article betrayed a long-standing skepticism. Over the past few years, Glaser has been advancing the message in major news organs that twelve-step programs are bad for everyone, including women (*Wall Street Journal*), teenagers (*New York Times*), heroin addicts (*The Daily Beast*), South Africans (*Marie Claire*), and doctors (*Daily Beast* again). But at eight thousand words, the *Atlantic* article was longer and received far more attention than did her earlier articles. It also offered the most complete formulation of her case. "The problem is that nothing about the 12-step approach draws on modern science," Glaser wrote, "not the character building, not the tough love, not even the standard 28-day rehab stay." If alcoholism is truly a disease, why is the default treatment a spiritually oriented support group run by nonprofessionals?

The story brought to the surface long-harbored suspicions about the idiosyncrasies of AA: its tent-meeting lexicon, the curious symmetry between the twelve steps and the twelve apostles, the whiff of secrecy and anonymity, the catacombic meeting spaces. During Glaser's media tour following the article's publication, news anchors and radio hosts were eager to connect the dots in places where the article had doubtlessly been constrained by fact-checkers. ("Let's go conspiracy theory just for a moment," said one radio host.) Glaser played her part by referring to the text *Alcoholics Anonymous* as AA's "bible" and by claiming that members were ordered off their psychiatric drugs and forbidden from consulting doctors. When one host asked her to impart some closing words, she spoke as though voicing a public service announcement: "If you are concerned about your drinking, it is really helpful to say to yourself, *You can change your drinking yourself. You have agency; you have control over it.*"

When Glaser's interviewers began citing counterarguments, Glaser responded with science: not, that is, with statistics or data, but literally with the word "science." "Epiphanies are not science," she remarked in response to the claim that AA's religious focus could be helpful. In reply to the observation that AA has worked for a lot of people, she said, "But that's not science. That's anecdote." Then she resorted to anecdote herself: "Hundreds of people have written to me to say that they were ordered off their meds by their sponsor for their mood disorder." On NPR's *All Things Considered*, she dropped her voice and spoke in a breathless, confiding tone: "Someone sent me an email this morning about a younger brother who committed suicide last night with the [AA] Big Book and a glass of scotch next to his bed."

All of this might be dismissed as an isolated media event— another story to satisfy our wolfish hunger for seeing respected institutions tarnished by scandal and exposé. But attitudes toward addiction, which Aristotle called one of the "irrational passions," have long offered a revealing window into cultural assumptions about human behavior. And although Glaser often presented herself as a voice in the wilderness, she is not the only one who has felt compelled to deliver the inconvenient truth about AA. Last year, Dr. Lance Dodes, a retired Harvard psychiatry professor, published *The Sober Truth: Debunking the Bad Science Behind 12-Step Programs and the Rehab Industry*, which he co-wrote with his son Zachary. More recently, Dr. Markus Heilig, of the National Institute on Alcohol Abuse and Alcoholism (NIAAA), echoed Glaser's call for more "evidence-based" treatment in *The Thirteenth Step: Addiction in the Age of Brain Science*. AA has attracted critics since its inception, but these authors constitute something of a new breed, and their work shares a central thesis: while AA maintains a special place in the American imagination, the data is clear that it simply doesn't work.

This charge is, it turns out, easy enough to refute; what makes these books worth pausing over is the sensibility that motivates them. Beneath the number crunching and the medical jargon lies the conviction that AA is not just ineffective but incoherent, repellent even. In the end, the most recent skirmish in the long quarrel between AA and its "scientific" critics hinges upon a question of human agency: Can the individual really—as Glaser alleges—help herself?

Alcoholics Anonymous's recent critics are united in presuming that science has not yet been harnessed for the treatment of addiction. In fact, scientists have been probing at alcoholism since before the Progressive Era. In 1870 inebriety was officially pronounced a "disease" by the American Association for the Study and Cure of Inebriety, an institution that declared, somewhat prematurely, that alcoholism was "curable in the same sense that other diseases are." Of course, the "cures" were rarely effective; some were actually dangerous. For nearly a century, hydrotherapy was the leading treatment for alcoholism. Nurses would wrap the detoxifying patient in cold, wet sheets, swaddling him for many hours. If that didn't work, the drunkard might be subject to an electric light bath, a method used by almost all of the leading hospitals of the world. This technique required locking the patient in a steel box, the inside of which was lined with plate mirrors, dozens of light bulbs, and steam coils to produce a sauna-like atmosphere. Medical authorities believed the light would purge "alcoholic germs" from the patient's cutaneous tissue. This is to say nothing of prefrontal lobotomy, spinal puncture, colonic irrigation therapy, or the dozens of other addiction treatments carried out over the last century in the name of science.

Medication, likewise, is hardly a new proposal for alcoholics. Throughout the nineteenth and early twentieth centuries, newspapers advertised a panoply of commercial tonics: the Fittz Cure, the Bellinger Cure, and the Tiplicuro. The most famous was Dr. Leslie Keeley's Double Chloride of Gold Cure, a remedy composed of strychnine, cocaine, codeine, and morphine that was given to over half a million alcoholics between 1880 and 1920. Many of these medications were the products of

charlatans—country quacks hoping to get rich off the cures—
but the drugs recommended by the leading medical institutions offered little improvement over the commercial remedies.
The Progressive Era was characterized by a frantic search for an
alcoholism "vaccine"—one was made from the blood of horses
that had been fed buckets of whiskey—and the twentieth century witnessed faddish experiments in "aversion therapy," giving alcoholics drugs that would make them violently ill when
they drank. Some of these aversion drugs are still on the market
today (Antabuse is the most popular), though there is little
evidence of their efficacy.

From the beginning, some alcoholics sought alternative routes to recovery. In his history of addiction treatment
in America, *Slaying the Dragon*, William L. White notes that
throughout the nineteenth and early twentieth centuries many
alcoholics banded together and offered one another support
through a variety of mutual aid societies like the Washingto-
nian Total Abstinence Society, a fellowship of working-class
men founded in the 1840s that held gatherings resembling
a contemporary AA meeting. Members signed an abstinence
pledge and told the story of their reform from a podium, drawing from the camp-meeting tradition of "experience sharing." At the height of the movement there were more than
600,000 members throughout the United States; Abraham
Lincoln, though a lifelong abstainer, was a vocal supporter of
the program.

Some fellowships, like Dr. Henry A. Reynolds's clubs, were
offshoots of temperance societies for those "addicted to strong
drink." Others grew out of fraternal orders. The Sons of Temperance was formed to address the need for mutual accountability and moral support. As one member put it, "a society
was, therefore, needed which should offer a refuge to reformed

men and shield them from temptation." These were far from sparsely populated fringe movements: during the 1850s, the Sons of Temperance boasted 250,000 members, with chapters in every state. Like the Washingtonians, these groups emphasized experience sharing and provided a haven for reformed drinkers within a culture that still stigmatized addiction as a moral vice. Many of the personal testimonies demonstrate a surprisingly contemporary understanding of alcoholism as neither a moral deficiency nor a sign of poor education. In his speeches, Dr. Reynolds would often call attention to his knowledge as a physician, on the one hand, and his inability to control his own drinking, on the other: "I am a graduate of Harvard College, and received a thorough medical education, but I have been drunk four times a day in my office, and if there is any worse hell than I have suffered I don't want to be there."

The popularity of such fellowships was undoubtedly fueled by the fact that professional medical treatments were so unhelpful. But these societies also sought to address addiction in ways that extended beyond the scope of medicine. Many were viewed as part of a "continuum of care." While medical treatment was naturally isolating, taking patients away from their families, the fellowships provided a community to belong to once the work of the hospitals—detoxification and stabilization—was finished. The goal was to equip the alcoholic with the moral clarity needed to set things right with themselves and their social circles. Some, like the Washingtonians, even maintained a pool of money for the purpose of helping newcomers pay off their debts and court fees.

Many of these organizations dissolved during Prohibition, and by the 1930s there were few remaining mutual aid societies. Like many wealthy alcoholics of that era, Bill Wilson, AA's founder, spent much of his adult life receiving the latest and most expensive medical treatments, including hydrotherapy and the famous belladonna cure, an acrid cocktail of prickly ash and the hallucinogen nightshade. It was while taking belladonna at Towns Hospital in Manhattan that Wilson underwent his famous conversion experience. He saw a bright light and felt he was in the presence of God. "Scales of pride and prejudice fell from my eyes," he recalls in the Big Book. "A new world came into view."

During the early months of his sobriety, Wilson often returned to Towns Hospital and asked to speak to the patients. It was there that he realized his urge to drink subsided when he was talking to other suffering alcoholics. "It was not just a case of trying to *help* alcoholics," he wrote years later. "If my own sobriety were to be maintained, I *had* to find another alcoholic to work with." As he began to sober up fellow patients, they too followed his method of working with other alcoholics. By 1939 there were a hundred men and women involved in this informal fellowship, and Bill began to devise a program of recovery based on the principle of "one alcoholic working with another."

Alcoholics Anonymous is notoriously difficult to evaluate scientifically. Several observational studies have been quite favorable to the program—finding, for instance, that the longer people attend twelve-step meetings, the more likely they are to achieve long-term sobriety, or that *engagement* in meetings, as opposed to mere attendance, can be correlated with sobriety. But for many, such studies are innately compromised by the fact that their members self-select. In *The Sober Truth*, Lance Dodes dismisses the observational studies wholesale. The kinds of people who go to AA—moreover, the ones who stick around—are those who find it useful. What about everyone else? To really understand the effectiveness of AA, Dodes suggests, we must consider everyone who walks into the rooms, including those reluctant attendees who skulk into the back rows of speaker meetings, nod off during the Serenity Prayer, and never return. AA's literature claims that those who fail to fully participate in the twelve steps tend to relapse, but for Dodes such warnings are little more than community propaganda, a way of blaming the participant when the program fails them. "Imagine if similar claims were made in defense of an ineffective antibiotic," he writes.

As the comparison makes clear, Dodes conceives of AA as a "treatment" for alcoholism, a term that assumes patient passivity and is at odds with how members often describe the program—as a spiritual discipline that requires its participants to engage in a series of actions and rituals. Yet it is the discussion of attendance versus participation that lays the groundwork for Dodes's conclusion about AA's inefficacy. Citing data from the NIAAA that claims up to 31 percent of people who go to AA stick around for a year or more, Dodes then modifies those numbers to reflect attendance rather than involvement. If we include all the people who have attended at least one AA meeting but failed to get "actively involved"—according to one study, that number is around 79 percent—the success rate becomes significantly smaller. And because the NIAAA data does not specify how many of those attendees remained sober during their year of engagement, Dodes decides to dock the number an additional several percentage points for good measure. It is this gerrymandered set of data that leads Dodes to the conclusion that "roughly 5 to 8 percent of the total population of people who enter AA are able to achieve and maintain sobriety for longer than one year."

AA's low success rate compels Dodes to look for alternative treatment paths, and *The Sober Truth* is ultimately an argument for his specialized brand of "psychodynamic" therapy, which is built on the proposition that the addictive impulse can be traced back to a single source: the desire to reverse a sense of "overwhelming helplessness." According to this theory, AA's poor statistical showing should come as no surprise, given that the program reinforces the addict's sense of helplessness as opposed to combating it. The process of making amends, for instance, involves needless self-flagellation. Equally disturbing is the notion that addicts must rely on a higher power to stay sober, even if the step is interpreted, as it often is by AA's more secular members, as making the group itself into the higher power. "The problem persists," he writes. "Why can't this ultimate power lie within the addict?"

Glaser, who cites Dodes's research several times in her *Atlantic* article, asks the same question in her book-length treatment of the subject, *Her Best-Kept Secret: Why Women Drink—and How They Can Regain Control*. The book, which bills itself as a clarion call for "evidence-based" addiction treatment, insists that the twelve steps—such as admitting "powerlessness" and submitting one's will to a higher power—are particularly damaging to AA's female members. Glaser tells the stories of several affluent suburban women who summon the courage to attend a meeting only to discover that it's a massive downer. They don't like that abstinence is nonnegotiable. They are horrified by the prospect of uttering the words "I'm an alcoholic." They balk at the terms "powerlessness" and "surrender." In her *Atlantic* article Glaser tells the story of Jean, a floral designer whose physician recommends she try AA:

The whole idea made Jean uncomfortable. How did people get better by recounting the worst moments of their lives to strangers? Still, she went. Each member's story seemed worse than the last: One man had crashed his car into a telephone pole. Another described his abusive blackouts. One woman carried the guilt of having a child with fetal alcohol syndrome. "Everybody talked about their 'alcoholic brain' and how their 'disease' made them act," Jean told me. She couldn't relate. She didn't believe her affection for pinot noir was a disease, and she bristled at the lines people read from the Big Book: "We thought we could find a softer, easier way," they recited. "But we could not." Surely, Jean thought, modern medicine had to offer a more current form of help.

Much of AA's philosophy is built on the principle of "identification"—seeing yourself in the stories of others—with newcomers like Jean being encouraged to "look for the similarities." But according to Glaser, identification is precisely the problem. One of her favorite ways to criticize AA is to refer to its "one-size-fits-all" approach. Evidence-based treatment, in her view, should treat each alcoholic as a unique case, helping her discover the cause of her own drinking and developing customized recovery goals, whether the aim is abstinence or moderation. And it is this mode of treatment that distinguishes Your Empowering Solutions (YES), a treatment center on the Palos Verdes Peninsula, California, for which Glaser reserves her most ebullient praise.

The chapter on YES, entitled "Twenty-First-Century Treatment," follows the story of Joanna, a mezzo-soprano who enrolls at a time when she has been drinking roughly three liters of chardonnay a day. Joanna is immediately impressed by the "bright, modern office," the friendly staff, and the positive vibes ("even the magazines were upbeat"). She's given a personalized therapy regime, which consists mostly of discussing her life goals with her psychiatrists—a technique called "motivational interviewing"—though she also takes a lot of long walks on the beach, listens to meditation CDs, and eats big salads at local cafés with her two psychiatrists. "There was no dining hall, no other patients she had to make small talk with: just Joanna and her two shrinks." During her treatment, Joanna comes to a series of realizations, including the epiphany that drinking is preventing her from using her leisure time efficiently. "In addition to adding more exercise and eating better, she wanted to finish decorating her master bedroom, organize her belongings better, and hang pictures that had been sidelined next to the wall for years." She leaves the center at the end of the week with a customized treatment plan and a prescription for naltrexone, an opioid antagonist Glaser claims can help alcoholics drink in moderation. "As she returned to Pennsylvania, she felt armed with knowledge—about herself, her personal development, and the vision she had for her life."

The reader is left to wonder why a woman who decided to spend $10,000 on addiction treatment needed a doctor to help her realize drinking was interfering with her life. But Glaser's case studies are rife with simplistic moments of revelation. Many of the women she writes about find help via online recovery programs that rely on cost-benefit analysis to show users how their drinking is irrational. Fully autonomous and empowered by data, these women rigorously check their stats and make adjustments accordingly, sometimes aided by doctors who are less figures of medical authority than hired number crunchers or benign spirit guides, facilitating their personal journey. When Jean, the floral designer, returns to the bottle, Glaser proudly notes that her doctor "calls this 'research,' not 'a relapse.'" (Members of twelve-step programs also refer to relapses as "doing more research," though the tone is notably less sunny: "I saw Bob's car outside the liquor store this morning. Guess he went out to do some more research.")

If addicts are engaging in behavior that is detrimental to their interests, Glaser insists, it must be because they lack the information or insight to make educated choices. The same conviction lies behind a spate of new mobile apps for addicts— programs like recoveryBox, a toolset that enables users to track their behaviors each day, rating their anxiety and depression levels and categorizing each action as either "green" (taking medication, exercising), "yellow" (engaging with triggers), or "red" (relapse). Based on these self-reported actions, the application will alert the user when he or she is entering a risk zone. "Breaking habits requires knowing why we do what we do, when do we do it and coming up with goals to break unhealthy behaviors," reads recoveryBox's website. A similar assumption underlies A-CHESS, a smartphone app for alcoholics that can track when the user is nearing a bar or tavern and alert their counselor. The app is said to reduce the risk of relapse by offering reminders that "encourage adherence to therapeutic goals" and providing users with "individualized addiction-related educational material."

For all the bluster about modern science, though, such approaches to addiction are far from original. Throughout early American history, alcoholics were exhorted to overcome addiction through willpower and sedulous self-monitoring. In fact, the charts and cost-benefit analyses Glaser recommends resemble nothing so much as puritan temperance tracts. These pamphlets, which bore titles like "Practical Facts for Practical

People," sought to reform addicts with ample doses of logos, arguing that drunkenness interfered with one's health and productivity. Some, like "The Cost of Beer," laid out the economic costs of drinking in precise dollar amounts, demonstrating that drunkenness was inefficient. These pamphlets and lectures amounted to little more than pep talks, but they were girded with the authority of science. Preachers peppered their sermons with quotes from scientists and doctors, and one of the leading early temperance organizations was called the Scientific Temperance Federation of Boston. The idea was that if people were informed about the costs of their bad decisions, then they would have no choice but to turn their lives around. It was precisely the failure of such methods that caused addicts to gravitate toward mutual aid societies like AA in the first place.

The promise of self-mastery has long occupied the American imagination. In "The Way to Wealth," a collection of maxims eventually added to his bestselling *Autobiography*, Benjamin Franklin offered rigorous self-scrutiny as a method for curtailing vice and achieving commercial success. A century later the transcendentalists, led by Emerson and Thoreau, would privilege the virtues of "self-reliance" over ties to any community, tradition, or institutional authority. ("Trust thyself," boomed Emerson: "every heart vibrates to that iron string.") Closer to the time of AA's founding, the American individualist creed had trickled down into the works of popular self-help gurus like William Walker Atkinson, whose 1906 book *Thought Vibration* held that "every man has, potentially, a strong Will, and . . . all he has to do is to train his mind to make use of it."

It is no accident that Alcoholics Anonymous originated during the 1930s, at a time when the deprivations of the Great

Depression caused Americans to question many of their long-held assumptions about such matters. The sociologist Robin Room has noted that the program's philosophy deeply resonated with the generation of men whose motto "I am the master of my fate, / I am the captain of my soul" had failed to protect them from economic calamity. AA's founder, Bill Wilson, was a stockbroker whose personal nadir coincided with the crash of the market, and in his autobiographical writings he often conflated the failure of this national ideology with his inability to master his own drinking. "A morning paper told me the market had gone to hell again," he wrote of a relapse in 1932. "Well, so had I."

Shortly after his spiritual transformation, Wilson read William James's *The Varieties of Religious Experience*, a book that offered a humble alternative to the prevailing ethos of self-determination. James believed that American life was marked by "over-tension," a vestige of the Protestant work ethic. "Official moralists advise us never to relax our strenuousness," he writes. "'Be vigilant, day and night,' they adjure us; 'hold your passive tendencies in check; shrink from no effort; keep your will like a bow always bent.'" For James, this obsessive self-monitoring leads to an impasse of the will, a continuous battle between the spirit and the flesh. It was not modern science but rather ancient religion that provided James with the imagery he would use to describe these warring desires. He found in the works of spiritual writers repeated examples of the condition he called "the divided self." The words of the apostle Paul were emblematic: "I do not understand my own actions. For I do not do what I want, but I do the very thing I hate."

James believed that for individuals who were enslaved by such a condition, no amount of rationalizing could help: "Peace cannot be reached by the simple addition of pluses and elimination of minuses from life." The divided self, he argued, could be made whole only through an anti-moralistic method, a process of surrender that reoriented the attention onto an external objective, thereby transcending the old, rigid patterns of thinking:

> Give up the feeling of responsibility, let go your hold, resign the care of your destiny to higher powers, be genuinely indifferent as to what becomes of it all, and you will find not only that you gain a perfect inward relief, but often also, in addition, the particular goods you sincerely thought you were renouncing. This is the salvation through self-despair, the dying to be truly born. . . . To get to it, a critical point must usually be passed, a corner turned within one. Something must give way, a native hardness must break down and liquefy; and this event (as we shall abundantly see hereafter) is frequently sudden and automatic, and leaves on the Subject an impression that he has been wrought on by an external power.

The idea of the sundered self resonated with Wilson, who had been baffled by his own "incredible behavior in the face of a desperate desire to stop." His own Iliad of addiction, which appears in the first chapter of *Alcoholics Anonymous*, reverberates in the personal narratives that appear in the book's subsequent pages. The alcoholic comes up with rational theories about his drinking and embarks on experiments designed to master it: drinking only beer, exercising more, going to psychoanalysis. "But there was always the curious mental phenomenon," Wilson writes, "that parallel with our sound reasoning there inevitably ran some insanely trivial excuse for taking the first drink. Our sound reasoning failed to hold us in check. The insane idea won out." To be an alcoholic, Wilson argues, is to confront the essentially irrational side of one's nature. Looking deeply into the self only draws one further into the realm of the absurd.

In order to escape the endless cycle, the addict had to train his or her gaze away from the self, directing it toward a higher power and the still-suffering alcoholic. This concept was, as much as the program's spiritual emphasis, an application of James's ideas (later in life, Wilson would claim that James was "one of our founders"): rather than focusing on one's own internal war, the alcoholic externalized that struggle by working with another man who was worse off. Those who complain that the program is run by "nonprofessionals" often miss the fact that, according to Wilson's model, the primary beneficiary is the provider of aid, not its receiver. AA has often been labeled a "self-help group," but it is in fact the opposite: a fellowship for people who have utterly failed in their attempts to help themselves.

When *Alcoholics Anonymous* was published in 1939, the American Medical Association declared it to have "no scientific merit or interest," while the *Journal of Nervous and Mental Disease* called it a "rambling sort of camp meeting confession of experience." Such perspectives, which resemble those taken by Dodes and Glaser, continue to find a sympathetic audience today, when confessing to being powerless over anything is regarded as a defeatist attitude starkly at odds with the mandate to better oneself through data and information. In fact, belief in the mantras of scientific self-empowerment is so strong that it often persists even when science itself seems to indicate what AA has always suggested: that the conviction that we can take control over our lives is—especially for addicts—largely an illusion.

Indeed many neurologists now believe alcoholism is a brain disease that inhibits precisely the sort of "rational" thinking Glaser and Dodes insist upon. This is the contention of Markus Heilig, of the National Institute on Alcohol Abuse and Alcoholism. Heilig holds a PhD in psychiatric neurochemistry and has spent two decades working with alcoholics. Although there's no indication that he has read Dodes or Glaser, the first chapters of his book *The Thirteenth Step* read like a bald refutation of their theories. Heilig thinks it is a mistake to encourage alcoholics to moderate or psychoanalyze their behavior; the whole point is that the addict lacks self-control. In fact Heilig goes further, dismissing the very notion of free will in a breezy eight-page chapter relaying the "astonishing" hypothesis that human beings are, in the words of Nobel laureate Francis Crick, "no more than the behavior of a vast assembly of nerve cells and their associated molecules."

One would think that Heilig's biological materialism would make him partial to drug-related treatments for addiction. But while much of Heilig's book is spent discussing the promise of such pills, he argues that medication is a long way from being able to address alcoholism in its full complexity, since (unlike other addictions) it does not interact with a specific brain receptor. Until the drug situation improves, Heilig recommends cognitive behavioral therapy. This includes strategies such as "fishbowl reinforcement," in which clean urinalyses are rewarded by granting the addict the privilege of reaching into a glass fishbowl to retrieve a slip of paper that says "Good job!" or promises a small cash reward, and other methods like encouraging the addict to write a "set of screenplays" to help her avoid "relapse triggers." "Use your creativity to develop what that alternative plot will be," Heilig advises, "because it has to be one that works for you, and you are the expert on your own life."

Aside from the sheer silliness of such methods, a paradox lurks in Heilig's logic. Aren't such strategies a contradiction in terms for someone who doesn't believe in free will? Heilig has considered this objection. While personal choice remains an illusion, he argues, recovery depends, conversely, upon the patient's *belief* in their ability to choose, a concept he calls "self-efficacy": "To get to their goals, people need to feel that they have an ability to influence the course of their lives." Of the inconsistency in this reasoning, Heilig writes:

> I don't know how to theoretically reconcile an understanding of the brain as a machinery that produces behavior based on the laws of nature, on one hand, with a view of the brain's owner as an agent endowed with a free will to choose one behavior over another, on the other. It does not seem that anyone else knows the answer to this dilemma either, so I have decided not to worry too much about it for now.

Heilig's honesty is commendable, but it raises an obvious question: If the leading scientific experts contend that recovery from addiction depends upon belief in a fictional entity—free will—why is it any more "irrational" to believe in YHWH, the spirit of the universe, or the community of fellow alcoholics? If a fundamental barrier to recovery is distrust of one's "self-efficacy," wouldn't it make perfect sense for the addict to mentally project that fictional power onto an external entity to whom she can then appeal for help?

After his spiritual awakening, Bill Wilson was seized with fear that he was going mad. He had lost his desire to drink and felt he had experienced the presence of a higher power, but he also considered the possibility that he'd had a hallucination. When he described the experience to his doctor, the physician responded with an air of suspended disbelief. "Something has happened to you I don't understand," he told Wilson, "but you had better hang on to it." It was this moment—rather than the spiritual experience itself—that Wilson would credit with saving his life. "If he had said 'hallucination,'" he wrote years later, "I might now be dead."

That physician, Dr. William D. Silkworth, would become a lifelong advocate for AA. When the Big Book was published, he wrote an introduction entitled "The Doctor's Opinion." The introduction is offered as a medical perspective on alcoholism, but Silkworth spends much of the chapter speaking of the limits of his own profession when it comes to curing addiction. "We doctors have realized for a long time that some form of moral psychology was of urgent importance to alcoholics," he wrote, "but its application presented difficulties beyond our conception. What with our ultra-modern standards, our scientific approach to everything, we are perhaps not well equipped to apply the powers of good that lie outside our synthetic knowledge." While Silkworth's classification of AA as a form of "moral psychology" betrays some uneasiness with the program's spiritual rhetoric, what ultimately convinced him was the evidence of the lives he'd seen changed. "We feel, after many years of experience, that we have found nothing which has contributed more to the rehabilitation of these men than the altruistic movement now growing up among them," he wrote. The sentiment shares a bloodline with the pragmatism of William James, who held that "we cannot reject any hypothesis if consequences useful to life flow from it."

So useful were the contributions of AA that, by the early 1960s, the program had grown to a membership of over 120,000 in the United States, with more than 8,000 groups around the world. Perhaps these numbers gave Wilson the confidence to seek out another luminary in the scientific community—Carl Jung. Wilson noted in his first letter to Jung that the psychiatrist's writings were popular among AA members. "Because of your conviction that man is something more than intellect, emotion, and two dollars' worth of chemicals, you have especially endeared yourself to us," he wrote. But Wilson was writing primarily in regards to a mutual acquaintance named Rowland H., a former patient of Jung's who had been pronounced "incurable." Wilson announced that Rowland had since undergone a spiritual awakening, gotten sober, and played a prominent role in the founding of AA.

Jung responded to the news with enthusiasm. He'd long suspected that experiences of this kind could have such an effect on alcoholics, but the nature of his profession prevented him from prescribing a spiritual solution. "The use of such words arouse so many mistakes that one can only stay aloof from them as much as possible," he writes. "These are the reasons why I could not give a full and sufficient explanation to Rowland H., but I am risking it with you." Jung proceeds to describe, in halting terms, the path by which one may experience such a transformation, led by "an act of grace, or through personal and honest contact with friends, or through a high education of the mind beyond the confines of mere rationalism."

Jung admits that these concepts don't roll easily off his

tongue, that the language of his profession—of modernity in general—isn't adequate to his curiosity. "How," he asks, "could one formulate such an insight in a language that is not misunderstood in our days?" Perhaps Jung was speaking from experience. His own work often fell outside the boundaries of what was conventionally accepted as science, and he was no doubt familiar with his colleagues' tendency to marginalize what they did not understand. But his reluctance to dismiss AA embodies the very skepticism that is supposed to lie at the heart of the scientific endeavor—a willingness to interrogate one's own methods and, when necessary, to admit their limitations. When it comes to a province of human nature so elusive and vexed, we might do well to embrace such sobriety.

2016, *The Point*

MIDWESTWORLD

It was the kind of day in Detroit, late in the course of a temperate summer, when the heat rebounds and the humidity returns with a vengeance. We drove in on the freeway, past marshland and inoperative steel mills and townships whose names—Romulus, Troy—recalled the imperial ambitions of a more hopeful era. We were headed not to the city but to the simulation: the reconstructed historic town known as Greenfield Village. At nine, when we arrived—my mother, my sisters, the children, and I—the parking lot was already packed. School had started a couple weeks earlier, and it appeared as though districts across the metro area had chosen the day for their inaugural field trip. Children poured out of Detroit Public Schools buses and shuttles stamped with the logos of Jewish day schools. There were Syrian and Yemeni kids from the Dearborn schools and kindergarteners dressed in the Hogwartian uniforms of parochial academies—all of them boundless and boisterous and shepherded by adults who bore the unexpressive fatalism of people who work professionally with children.

Saddled with diaper bags and water bottles, three small children in tow, we joined the throng at the gates and were promptly ushered into another world. Women in bonnets strolled down the thoroughfare. We passed tinsmith shops, farmhouses, horse-drawn buggies, and a man who had been paid, in the name of historical authenticity, to stand in a shadowless field in three layers of tweed, pretending to pick beans. We had come here, supposedly, for the children, who belonged to my two sisters, though we were really here for my mother, who was in the delirious throes of early grandmotherhood and insisted that this was a family tradition. She led the way with the kids, while my sisters and I lagged behind, each of us pushing an empty stroller and redundantly lamenting the heat. We had, in fact, loved this place when we were young, but as adults we became uncharacteristically cynical each time we returned, eager to call attention to the park's lapses in verisimilitude: the milliner surreptitiously texting beneath her apron; the two men dressed as farmhands, believing themselves out of earshot, discussing cyberterrorism as they forked hay into a wagon.

Greenfield Village describes itself as a "living history" museum. Unlike most museums, where artifacts are displayed in vitrines, the park is emphatically hands-on. Not only can you visit a nineteenth-century print shop where a man dressed in overalls operates a proof press with real ink; you can also attend one of the interactive workshops and make antique broadsides with your own two hands. On that summer morning, the Village was alive with the bustle of people making things. There were men tinkering in workshops, bent over bootjacks. There

were women in calico dresses pedaling flax wheels and knead-
ing actual bread dough to be baked in functional coal ovens.

The park, completed in 1929, was the vanity project of
Henry Ford, a man who years earlier had declared that "history
is more or less bunk." Later, he would clarify: *written* history
was bunk, because it focused on politicians and military heroes
rather than on the common men who built America. Greenfield
Village was his correction to the historical narrative. It was a
place designed to celebrate the inventor, the farmer, and the
agrarian landscape that had given rise to self-made men like
him. Ford had a number of historically significant buildings
relocated to the park, including the Wright brothers' cycle shop
and Thomas Edison's laboratory, both of which still stand on its
grounds. But the park was never really about history—not, at
least, in any objective sense. It was a sentimental re-creation of
the landscape of Ford's boyhood. To this day, patrons can visit
his family homestead, the one-room schoolhouse he attended,
and the workshop where he built his first car, buildings he not
only relocated to the park but also faithfully outfitted with the
decorative props he recalled from his youth.

Ford was evidently not alone in his longing for this bygone
era. The park's opening coincided with the Great Depression,
a time when many people felt disillusioned with modernity
and its narratives about progress. The Village, which evoked a
way of life recent enough to have persisted in the memories of
older visitors, attracted scores of Americans who felt alienated
from the land because of urbanization and factory work, and
who longed to return, if only momentarily, to the slower, more
satisfying pace of preindustrial life. In the forties, park guides
began their tours by encouraging patrons to "forget the hustle
and bustle of the atomic age and return briefly to the simple,
rugged life" their forefathers knew. The irony, of course, was

that the way of life the park romanticized was precisely that which Ford had helped usher into obsolescence with the invention of the automobile and the modern factory. The Village was modernity's elegy for an America that no longer existed, built by its most illustrious titan of industry.

Now here we were, some eighty years later, at the coda of another economic downturn. Throughout the worst years of the recession, a crisis that hit Michigan particularly hard, Greenfield Village and its sister site, the Henry Ford Museum, had become more popular than ever. At a time when tourist attractions across Michigan were struggling just to keep their doors open, the Village saw a surge in attendance. This was the first time I'd been back since the financial crisis, and I'd never seen the park so crowded. We spent most of the morning standing in lines, uselessly fanning ourselves with park brochures. At the machine shop, we waited almost an hour so that my niece could use a turret lathe to make a brass candlestick. It was a tedious process that involved several complicated steps, each of which was accompanied by the docent's plodding commentary. In the end, though, there was something undeniably satisfying in seeing raw material transformed into a concrete object. I remarked to my sister, as we watched her daughter operate the lathe, that it must be some comfort knowing that if the whole global infrastructure collapsed, at least one person in the family would be able to make decorative metalwork.

"It's character building," she replied.

There was, certainly, a moral aspect to these demonstrations. As the costumed docents explained each archaic skill, they stressed the time and care that went into each of these primitive crafts. The park seemed designed to be not only educational but also edifying; children were brought here so they could become acquainted with all manner of "traditional" virtues—hard work, diligence, collaboration, perseverance—whose relevance to our current economy was not, it occurred to me, entirely apparent. But maybe that was the point. If the park still persisted as a site of nostalgia, it was because it satisfied a more contemporary desire: to see a market that depended on the exchange of tangible goods, a world in which one's labor resulted in predictable outcomes and the health of the economy relied on a vast collaborative workshop powered by the sweat of common people. There are, of course, different kinds of nostalgia, some more flexible than others. On that day, there was a restive energy throughout the park, as though the collective longing that had brought us here was undergirded by something more desperate.

It is difficult, in a place like Detroit, to avoid thinking about the past. The city is still associated with an industry that peaked in the middle of the last century and has since succumbed to all the familiar culprits of urban decline—globalization, automation, disinvestment, and a host of racist public policies. Perhaps it was destined from the start to collapse beneath the weight of the metaphorical import placed on its shoulders. During the Depression and throughout the years leading up to World War II, the city stood as a symbol of national strength, a thrumming life force pumping blood into the economy—associations that persist in the city's epithets (the "arsenal of democracy") and its industries' ad campaigns (the "Heartbeat of America"). For decades, the auto industry boasted the highest-paid blue-collar jobs in America, making Detroit a magnet for working people from all over the country.

Among the first waves of migrants was my great-grandfather, who in the twenties abandoned his family's tobacco farm in southern Kentucky to build Model Ts for the wage of five dollars a day. His son, my grandfather, grew up on Warren Avenue during the Depression, shoveling coal for nickels to help with his family's expenses. These men, father and son, remained lucid and hale well into my adolescence. Between the two of them, plus a coterie of uncles who had given their best years to Chrysler, my childhood was steeped in nostalgia for the city's glory years. Hardly a family holiday went by when my siblings and I were not made to remain at the table after the food had been cleared to listen to their recollections of the city. "They used to call us the Paris of the Midwest," my grandfather would say. These were men who spoke of Henry Ford as a demigod, and for whom work, with all its attendant Protestant virtues, was a kind of religion. Their stories expressed a longing for a time when the country still relied on the brawn of men like themselves who had, despite coming from humble origins and not going to college, managed to lift their families into the middle class. But they were also meant for us children, the beneficiaries of all that hard work, whom they perhaps feared were growing up a little too comfortably in suburban exile.

From time to time, my grandfather would load us kids—my brothers and sisters and I—into the back of his Town Car and drive us downtown to see his old neighborhood. By the late nineties, the area was a characteristic stretch of bricked-over storefronts and condemned buildings, but it had once been a thriving residential area built for the city's auto workers, a neighborhood of single-family homes where southern transplants like his family lived alongside immigrants from Mexico, Poland, and Greece. "People came here from all over the world," he told us. "Everyone lived together and got along." It was a remark he repeated every time he took us downtown, and one that seemed to me, even as a child, suspiciously rosy. In fact, the racial zoning laws that segregated the city were already in force during the decades he lived there. It's possible that he was being sentimental, infusing his recollections with the same sort of romanticism that had colored Ford's vision of his pastoral boyhood. But I think he was also deliberately refashioning these memories, the way one does when imparting lessons to children. He was not speaking to a historical reality so much as evoking an ideal, one that has long been associated with Detroit: it was a place where anyone—regardless of education, race, or how recently they had come to this country—could, through hard work, enter the middle class.

Nostalgia was on my mind that day as we walked along the dusty roads of Greenfield Village. The country was entering the home stretch of a historically tumultuous election season, one in which Detroit had been revived, once again, as a symbol. This time, in the imagination of Donald Trump, the city— along with places like Cleveland, Pittsburgh, and the Pennsylvania coal country—became an emblem of bungled trade deals and inept Washington bureaucrats, representing an America that had been left behind in an era of breakneck change. Pundits dubbed this the "politics of nostalgia," but it was a yearning that felt different from my grandfather's wistfulness for the city of his youth. To be sure, many of Trump's platform points echoed grievances that had been loitering for decades in the op-ed pages of the *Detroit Free Press* and at dinner tables across Wayne County. But on the campaign trail these arguments were fed by something new, the raw energy of conspiracy and xenophobic scapegoating—a melancholia that longed to resurrect not only the economic landscape of midcentury America but also its racial and gender hierarchies.

Throughout the summer, I had watched many of my family

members—men who, like my grandfather, had once extolled the city as a diverse and booming metropolis of yore—fall captive to these nativist reveries. If my sisters and I felt particularly uneasy about being at the Village that day, and more eager than usual to expose its artifice, it was because the park could, in some sense, be read as a lurid expression of that constituency's vision of a nation made great again: a world before globalization and the advent of civil rights; a time when black Americans were relegated to tenant farms and women were hidden within the narrow confines of galley kitchens.

But the park had taken pains to revamp its sites in an effort to preempt this more thorny form of nostalgia. Throughout the eighties and nineties, the Village amended its mission to offer a more progressive view of history. In place of Ford's celebration of self-made manhood, the sites now emphasized "community life." The bucolic romanticism of Ford's day had likewise been replaced with a focus on the shifting technological landscape of nineteenth-century America and the innovations that led to the first wave of the Industrial Revolution. The Village had become, in the words of its former president, "the great American museum of change." An African-American Cultures program was added to address the history of racial injustice inherent in the park's representations of the past, and the guide scripts had been expanded to highlight the contributions of immigrants, minorities, and women.

Some of these revisions were a bit of a stretch. At the general store, a female docent showed my sisters and me an early wholesale catalog and insisted that women's demand for consumer goods significantly shaped the economic landscape of the nineteenth century. I turned to my sisters to impart some ironic remark and was surprised to find them listening with attentiveness. By this point, we had caught up with my mom and the kids, and my sisters had become mothers again. They were watching the faces of their daughters; it is difficult to be cynical in the presence of children. We were, on that day, among hundreds of them—kids who had come from all parts of the city to learn about their nation's history—and the park docents were doing their best to impart a version of that story that included everyone. If nothing else, we owed them this attempt.

In her 2001 book *The Future of Nostalgia*, the critic Svetlana Boym, who grew up in the Soviet Union, traces the different forms of nostalgia that emerged in post-communist Europe. Boym argues that the word's two Greek roots—*nostos*, or "the return home," and *algia*, or "longing"—embody two types of nostalgia that tend to arise in modern cultures: "reflective nostalgia" and "restorative nostalgia." Reflective nostalgia thrives on the feeling of longing. As much as it might idealize or romanticize the past, it is a flexible form of nostalgia that interacts, in creative ways, with the present and the future. Much like the revised narratives of Greenfield Village, or my grandfather's memories of Detroit, this brand of wistfulness is aware on some level that its visions of the past are illusory.

Restorative nostalgia, on the other hand, dwells in the feeling of *nostos*—"returning home." It seeks not only to remember the lost homeland, but also to rebuild it. This more rigid orientation toward the past lies at the root of nationalist movements, and unlike reflective nostalgia, which can be ironic or playful, it tends to be severe, if not authoritarian. Those who are drawn to this kind of nostalgia, Boym notes, "do not think of themselves as nostalgic; they believe that their project is about truth." Rather than meditating on the sense of loss, restorative movements exploit this longing by blaming certain groups of people who have supposedly caused the loss of the homeland. The Nazi pogroms, Stalin's Terror, and McCarthy's Red Scare, Boym argues, all appealed to restorative accounts of history. Such narratives are often fueled by conspiracy theories and a mythology of persecution.

Nostalgia almost always stems from an anxiety about modernity: the fear that progress is happening too fast, and that the past will be irrevocably lost. But restorative tendencies are more likely to emerge during especially dramatic periods of upheaval. Restorative movements often take root in the aftermath of revolutions, though they are also common during times of social and economic turbulence, particularly those that unsettle existing narratives about national identity. It is in such times, when the distance between reality and myth becomes unbridgeable, that nostalgia can coarsen into resentment and people begin hunting for someone to blame.

Here in Michigan, it's hard not to sense that something fundamental shifted, or perhaps snapped, during the recession—not necessarily at its nadir, but during the years that followed, when the news touted the "recovery" of the market while people throughout the state continued to lose their homes and their jobs. Any lingering belief that Detroit stood as a symbol of the nation—that its prosperity and the rest of the country's were intertwined—was shattered in 2013 when the city declared bankruptcy the same week the Dow Jones and the S&P closed at record highs. The city had been through hard times before; but if the crisis had a particularly demoralizing effect this time around it was because it undermined, in a way that even the Great Depression had not, the populist myths that have long animated the region. There is an uneasiness here, a needling suspicion that the fruits of the economy do not correspond to the exertions of the nation's labor force; that prosperity, once envisioned by Diego Rivera as an endless collaborative assembly line stretching into the future, is now a closed loop that ordinary people are locked out of. From such desperation, the natural tendency to reflect can evolve into a misguided effort to restore.

By the time we left the general store, the heat had become oppressive. The children were growing fractious, and the docents, with their Victorian cheeriness, were beginning to seem sinister. We made our way to the center of the Village, where there was a restored carousel, and each of us chose a painted animal; the children shared an antique bench carved to look like a swan. As the carousel began moving, the pipe organ churned out a kaleidoscopic rendition of "After the Ball," and soon the Village, and its visions of the past, became a blur of green. On a gilded unicorn, a man in a United Auto Workers cap snapped a selfie with his unsmiling granddaughter. A mother idly straightened her daughter's hijab. Everyone looked extremely tired.

The music stopped and the carousel slowed. People began collecting their bags and sliding their children off the wooden animals, but then the platform jolted and the carousel kicked back into gear. "Not over yet!" someone exclaimed. The man with the UAW cap joked about getting a two-for-one, and it became apparent that he was right: the ride seemed to have started over again. The organ played "After the Ball" from the beginning, though the tempo seemed slower this time and the melody began to warble, as though it were slipping into a minor key. As we wheeled around toward the operator box, I tried to determine whether anyone was manning the controls, but it was impossible to see inside. The other passengers seemed blithely resigned to our fate. It was hot, and the spinning created a welcome breeze. My mother was riding sidesaddle on a painted camel, texting. The children were narcotized, hair pasted against their temples, their eyelids weighted and fighting sleep. It was only when the music ended and we continued circling in silence that people began to look up with a dawning sense of alarm and seek out one another's gaze, as though everyone had collectively begun to wonder how we were going to get off.

2016, *The Point*

ON SUBTLETY

I.

In ancient Rome, there were certain fabrics so delicate and finely stitched they were called *subtilis*, literally "underwoven." The word—from which came the French *soutil* and the English *subtle*—often described the gossamer-like material that was used to make veils. I think of organza or the finest blends of silk chiffon, material that is opaque when gathered but sheer when stretched and translucent when held up to the light. Most wedding veils sold today use a special kind of tulle called Bridal Illusion, a term I've always loved, as it calls attention to the odd abracadabra of the veil, an accoutrement that is designed to simultaneously reveal and conceal.

II.

All writers have a chronic foible, a problem that tends to surface, again and again, in criticism of their work. Ever since I began writing, the adjective most frequently ascribed to my prose has been "subtle." When I wrote fiction, it was employed primarily as a compliment, though I suppose even then the term was double-edged. "One of the strengths of your writing is its subtlety." Thus began so many workshop transitions from praise to critique that hinged on the doubtful merit of that gift. My classmates were vocal about the many problems lurking in my stories: the character's motivation was not clear; the backstory should be addressed, not alluded to; the conclusion was too cryptic. At the time, I dismissed this as obtuseness. People wanted things spelled out. They weren't reading closely. But when I go back now and read those stories, it's clear that they were right. The clues I thought I had left for the reader are mere shadows, ghosts. There is almost nothing to hang on to.

There comes a point when a reproach is repeated so often it seems less a critique of your craft than an indictment of your character. For a long time, I worried what it said about me that my writing was subtle. I believed I was creating intellectual tension; I'd wanted to seduce the reader. But readers saw these tactics as cagey, as though I were ashamed of my ideas and trying to hide them behind a veil. For a while, everything I wrote seemed to hazard misinterpretation, inviting accusations of chicanery, purposelessness, or bad faith.

III.

We say that things are subtle when they are understated—as makeup or lighting—or when they are capable of making fine distinctions, as in a subtle mind. But the definition of "subtlety" that has long preoccupied me is that which means "indirect" or "concealed," and also its archaic definition ("cunning," "crafty"), which still haunts the contemporary meaning. "All literature is made of tricks," Borges once said. Some tricks, he noted, are easy enough to decipher, but the best ones are so sly they hardly feel like tricks at all. As a child homeschooled in an evangelical family, left to my own devices for great swaths of time, I became particularly good at uncovering the most obvious cues in a text. I knew that the poet meant for snow to symbolize death, or that a conversation between two people concerned abortion, even though the story never used the word. Literary interpretation is, essentially, a form of hermeneutics—a skill one learns osmotically from listening to sermons, a genre in which I was immersed. But the stories that captivated and unsettled me were those that remained irreducible. In these, there were no codes to be cracked, no definitive meaning to be exposed—just the faintest sense that the surface of the text was undergirded by a vast system of roots that must remain forever invisible.

Today, many of the smartest people I know have become infatuated with melodrama, genre fiction, and TV dramas: narratives that wear their ideas easily on their sleeve. "It is heavy-handed in the best way," writes a prominent magazine critic about a novel that has recently been serialized for television. "It makes everything blunter and more explicit, almost pulpy at times." It seems that all of us, exhausted by New Criticism, caught up in the throes of peak TV, have finally outgrown whatever charms the elusive once held. There exists among people my age a tendency to dismiss subtlety as "evasive" or "coy," as though whatever someone has taken pains to conceal must be somehow ill intentioned, cut from the same unwholesome cloth as dog-whistle politics and the silky doublespeak of reptiles like Richard Spencer. Perhaps the slogans of the Trump era have now extended themselves to the arts: we must speak in one voice, in no uncertain terms. Each week, I receive emails from any number of activist organizations that begin in more or less the same way: "Let me be clear . . ."

IV.

Being a Christian required an interpretive vigilance, a willingness to harken to whispers. As children, we were taught to remain alert at all times. God could speak to you through a fortune cookie, a highway billboard, the lyrics of pop songs. Fools could proclaim his wisdom, and radio DJs could be his angels in disguise. Once, during a long drive to a church retreat, our youth pastor pointed to the license plate of the car ahead of us and explained that each of its letters corresponded to a problem he'd been praying over for months. Interpretation slid easily into paranoia and faith into superstition, but the point was you had to pay attention. If you let your guard down you might miss the miracle, like the disciples at Gethsemane who fell asleep on their watch.

The problem was you could never be certain the signs were not from the darker forces. The devil too was subtle, according to the book of Genesis: "Now the serpent was more subtle than any beast of the field which the Lord God had made." (My mother, who dictated the passages my siblings and I committed to memory, preferred the King James Version, which rendered it *subtil.*) As a child, I often wondered what it meant that the devil was subtle. It was clear that he was mutable, appearing and disappearing throughout scripture in various disguises: as a snake, a lion, or an angel of light. More likely, though, it referred to his rhetoric, which was coy and Socratic. *Hath God said, Ye shall not eat of every tree of the garden?* A cruder entity would have made demands or arguments, but Lucifer wove elaborate traps of questions, prodding his victim to reach the relevant conclusion herself.

V.

Doris Lessing once complained that her novel *The Golden Notebook* was wildly misinterpreted. For her, the book was about the theme of "breakdown," and how madness was a process of healing the self's divisions. She placed this theme in the center of the novel, in a section that shared the title of the book, which she assumed would lead readers to understand that it was the cipher. Rather than making the themes explicit, she wanted to hint at them through the form of the novel itself, "to shape a book which would make its own comment, a wordless statement: to talk through the way it was shaped." But in the end, her efforts did not translate. "Nobody so much as noticed this central theme . . . ," she complained in the introduction to the 1971 edition. "Handing the manuscript to publisher and friends, I learned that I had written a tract about the sex war, and fast discovered that nothing I said then could change that diagnosis."

Ten years after the book was published, she claimed it was not uncommon to receive three letters in a single week, each of them offering three distinct interpretations: one reader wrote only about the theme of women's liberation; another had read it through a Marxist lens; the third was interested in the book as a treatise on mental illness. One might argue, as people often do, that these various readings testify to the book's complexity, but Lessing was unnerved by the reaction. "But it is the same book," she wrote. "And naturally these incidents bring up again questions of what people see when they read a book, and why one person sees one pattern and nothing at all of another pattern, and how odd it is to have, as author, such a clear picture of a book, that is seen differently by its readers."

It is not difficult to hear in her words a note of loneliness, one that echoes all those artists who have been woefully misunderstood: Lewis Carroll wrote *Alice's Adventures in Wonderland* as a protest against complex math. Georgia O'Keeffe insisted that her paintings of poppies and irises were not meant to evoke female genitalia (flowers, her defenders keep pointing out, fruitlessly, are androgynous). Ray Bradbury once claimed at a UCLA lecture that his novel *Fahrenheit 451* was not about censorship, but about the dangers of television. He was shouted out of the lecture hall. Nietzsche abhorred anti-Semitism, but when Hitler came across a copy of *On the Genealogy of Morals*, he interpreted the image of the "splendid blond beast" as a symbol of the Aryan race. One wonders what might have happened had Nietzsche simply written: "lion."

VI.

Christ himself was a master of the indirect, speaking in parables more often than in sermons. In their original form, as they appeared in the *logia*—the collection of his sayings that circulated before the writing of the Gospels—the parables have the tenor of riddles: A sower went out with a handful of seeds, scattering them across the earth. Some seeds fell on rocky soil, others fell on thorns, some were eaten up by birds before they could take root, but some found good soil and produced fruit. What does it mean? In the *logia*, Christ provides no guidance. Many of the stories end with the phrase "He who has ears to hear, let him hear." Another riddle, though most scholars believe it to mean: Let he who is capable of understanding these mysteries receive them.

When I was at Bible school, experiencing the first pangs of doubt, the subtlety of the gospel troubled me. The message of salvation should have been democratic, available to all. But it was not clear. Time and again, the disciples asked Jesus if he was the Son of God, and he refused to answer—or else gave some impossible reply: "Who do you say I am?" Was it not irresponsible that Christ had come to Earth with a handful of koans and esoteric stories and expected his message to be understood by the entire world? I once raised this question in a theology course. The professor opened the question to the class. When it became clear that nobody was going to answer, he took off his glasses and spoke with a quiet gravity. "One paradox has remained true throughout history," he said. "The more explicitly God reveals himself to mankind, the more likely we are to reject him. Christ did finally declare himself the Son of God, and we crucified him."

VII.

For as long as I can remember, I've had vivid and memorable dreams. They are often very beautiful, rendered in lush floral colors and almost cinematic in their level of detail. The only problem is that they are so relentlessly on the nose. When I turned thirty and my in-box was suddenly flooded with birth announcements, I had a recurring dream in which a tiny deformed man followed me around as I performed my daily rituals. I would be trying to brush my teeth, or walking to the store, and there was the little man waddling after me, waving amiably like a salesman trying to get my attention, so that I was forced to admonish him, beneath my breath, to go away. Another time, after I'd written something of which I was ashamed, I dreamt that I was sitting in my mother's kitchen being made to drink a vial of ink just as I'd been made to take cold medicine as a child. "Your dreams," my sister remarked once, "are like Freud for idiots."

If the purpose of dreams is to alert the conscious mind to what it has ignored or forgotten, then mine are very efficient— something for which I suppose I should be grateful. But I often wonder whether my subconscious isn't giving me too little credit. It is a strange thing to have your sensibilities so offended by your own dormant imagination. In the end, the obviousness of these messages makes me reluctant to heed them, as though doing so would only increase the grimy indignity of being pandered to.

VIII.

During those years of doubt, when God seemed distant or completely silent, I tried to remind myself that this was what it meant to be a bride of Christ. Earthly life was imbued with a kind of romantic tension; it was a cosmic game of seduction wherein our Creator played hard to get. If life seemed unjust, if God himself felt absent, it was because we were blinded, as humans, from seeing the unifying story that would emerge only at the end of time. Until that glorious wedding day, when the veil would be lifted and the truth would be revealed, the nature of reality must appear to us as shadows, like figures passing darkly across a clouded mirror.

When I finally abandoned my faith, I believed I was leaving this inscrutable world behind. I imagined myself exiting a primitive cave and striding onto terra firma, embracing a world where there would be no more shadows, no more distant echoes, only the blinding and unambiguous light of science and reason. But as it turns out, the material world is every bit as elusive as the superstitions I'd left behind. The laws of physics are slippery and resistant to grand unifying theories. The outcomes of quantum experiments change depending on our observation of them. Particles solidify when we probe them, but become waves when we turn our backs. As the physicist Paul Davies once put it, "nature seems to play tricks on us." Some scientists have now begun to take seriously the proposition that we exist within a multiverse, that we are forever separated from the truth of our existence by an impenetrable quantum veil.

What to make of this sly and nonsensical world that is indifferent to our curiosity? If the universe were a novel, we might say that it is "elusive," or perhaps even "opaque." If it were a god, we could only conclude that he had hidden his face. But perhaps it is a mistake—one common in our age of transparency—to perceive that which escapes our understanding as necessarily suspect. Others have found in these cosmic mysteries not tricks but signs of the ineffable. "The Lord God is subtle, but malicious he is not," said Albert Einstein. "Nature hides her secrets because of her essential loftiness, but not by means of ruse."

IX.

I worry, once again, that my oblique approach has managed only to muddle things. I suppose I've been trying to suggest that subtlety is always a sign of mystery, and that our attitude toward the former is roughly commensurate with our tolerance for the latter. I have come to regard it as something of a dark art, a force of nature that can be summoned but never fully harnessed, and can backfire at the slightest misstep. Anyone can pick up a bullhorn and make her intent clear to all, but to attempt something subtle is to step blindfolded into the unknown. You are always teetering on the brink of insanity. You are always working on a wire strung across an abyss, hoping to make it from one end to the other without losing your balance, or your mind.

Perhaps this is another way of saying that subtlety is a transaction of faith. The artist must have faith that her effects will be perceived in the way she intends; the reader must trust that what he detects, beneath the surface of the text, is not merely a figment of his imagination. The disciple must come to believe that the whispers he hears in the wilderness are not the wind, or the devil, but the voice of his Creator. All religion, all forms of love, depend on this leap.

2018, *Tin House*

THE END

In 1999 my family believed the world was coming to an end. We were living in central Wisconsin, on the outskirts of a lake district (my parents noted, more than once, the fortuitous proximity to sources of fresh water), and as the millennium neared, our house became a fortress braced for the apocalypse. Trucks arrived each week from Mountain House, a company that manufactures rations for the U.S. Special Forces and sells things like freeze-dried chicken and vacuum-sealed pouches of beef stew. I'd be doing chemistry homework or watching an episode of *Friends*, when my dad's voice would bellow out, "Mountain House!"—a boatswain's call designed to rally everyone to the driveway for unloading. Together we unloaded boxes from pallets and carried them down to the basement, which had been converted into a storeroom packed with generators, short-wave radios, shotguns, and a collection of fifty-five-gallon plastic drums for water storage, which my siblings and I occasionally borrowed for recreational rolls down the sloped hill of our backyard.

The panic was my parents' response to the Y2K bug, though its roots could be traced to an abiding occupation with biblical prophecy. They were among a handful of evangelicals who saw the computer glitch as the spark that could ignite the epic conflagration known as the end times, taking down the entire Western infrastructure and paving the way for the rise of the one-world government predicted in the book of Revelation. We would, ideally, survive on these provisions until the Rapture. That summer, my parents took us on a long-promised pilgrimage to Israel, where we climbed to the top of Mount Carmel. There, with dozens of other born-again tourists from around the world, we looked out at the Valley of Jezreel, an expanse of alluvial greenness where the Battle of Armageddon would take place.

Of course, the world did not end come January. For the remainder of my senior year, our family ate colorless suppers of dried meat and powdered mashed potatoes, refusing to speak about the error. I was off to Moody Bible Institute in the fall, but my sister claims that as late as 2008, our mom was still working through the dregs of that massive storeroom, trying to pass off the supplies as homemade meals. "It's just something I found in the pantry," she would say, upon which the entire table would drop their forks in horror and exclaim, "This is Y2K food, isn't it?!"

Like a lot of former believers, I often regard my childhood as having occurred in a parallel dimension, one that occupies the same physical coordinates as secular reality but operates according to none of its rules or logic. Other times, I am struck by the ordinariness of my experience. In the age of "superstorms" and

Ready.gov, it's not unusual for people to have a cache of bottled water in their basement, or to casually speculate about fending a hungry mob off their property. As my friends and I hover around the knell of thirty, childless and saddled with debt, we speak about the future with an almost welcome sense of contingency. "If the glaciers haven't melted," we say, or "when the singularity occurs," just as my parents couched every plan in the caveat "if the Lord tarries."

"We now live in a world shaped by evangelicals' apocalyptic hopes, dreams, and nightmares," Matthew Avery Sutton writes in *American Apocalypse: A History of Modern Evangelicalism*. While it's tempting to dismiss biblical fundamentalists as reactionaries, filtering current events through the lens of their bizarre theology, Sutton argues that the obverse is true: apocalypticism has been a potent force in our nation's history and has left an indelible mark on American political life.

Despite the ancient and primitive aura that is often attached to fundamentalism, the movement was both a response to and a product of modernity. Sutton's history begins at the height of the Progressive Era, a time of scientific and technological progress when most Americans believed that humanity was on a steady Hegelian trajectory toward perfection. Late nineteenth-century Christians were largely in tune with this optimism. They sought to fight corruption, alleviate poverty, and work toward social justice, believing that such social improvements would hasten the arrival of the Millennial Kingdom, the one thousand years of earthly peace and prosperity promised in the Bible, after which Christ would return. But progress is a weird thing; it has a way of engendering optimism and dysphoria in similar measure. In the glare of this dawning future, some believers retreated to their Bibles and found in its more obscure passages a darker vision of the future.

At the helm of this movement was John Nelson Darby, an Anglo-Irish preacher who concluded that his fellow Christians had been reading the Bible incorrectly; scripture clearly stated that Christ was going to return before, not after, the Millennial Kingdom. Preceding this Second Coming would be a period of tribulation: pestilence, natural disasters, and the rise of the Antichrist, a totalitarian leader who would wage war against Israel and rule over a coalition of nations in the former Roman Empire. Darby was drawing primarily from passages in Daniel, Ezekiel, and Revelation—Jewish apocalyptic literature that imaginatively envisioned the destruction of Jerusalem and wars between the empires of the ancient world. He believed these passages should be taken at face value, as references to the yet unrealized future. There was not, at that time, a nation of Israel, but this didn't bother him; God would bring the Jews back to Palestine at some point before the tribulation. This new theology was called premillennialism. It was a rather technical contention, but embedded in it was a radically new attitude toward earthly life: humanity was headed not toward utopia but to annihilation.

Darby's theory fell on rocky soil in Britain, but it did take root in the United States. His theology found a particularly sympathetic ear in the American evangelist Dwight L. Moody (the founder of my alma mater), who would become one of the fiercest proponents of premillennialism. By the early 1920s, this doctrine had created a schism within American Christianity, separating the new biblical conservatives—the self-described fundamentalists—from their liberal Protestant brethren. Fundamentalists withdrew from mainstream Christian culture, fortifying their own institutions such as Moody Bible Institute and the Bible Institute of Los Angeles.

Fundamentalism might have remained an obscure,

Gnostic-like offshoot of Christianity—something akin to Manichaeism—had the decades following its arrival in America not confirmed its pessimistic outlook. The two world wars, as well as the rise of fascism and bolshevism, seemed to validate the premillennial forecast of an abrupt and violent end, which attracted new converts to the movement. By the advent of the Cold War, preachers faced little difficulty tapping into the angst of an American public terrified at the prospect of nuclear annihilation. "Amid the disjuncture of modern times," Sutton writes, "apocalypticism often made better sense than competing theologies."

Because most Americans today associate end-times proclamations with the religious fringe—televangelists, street preachers—it's easy to underestimate the influence this theology has had in the halls of power. John D. Rockefeller and J. P. Morgan subscribed to premillennialism, as did William E. Blackstone, a Chicago real estate developer who wrote the 1878 bestseller *Jesus Is Coming*, and became one of the first advocates for the reestablishment of Israel. Over the past century, the fundamentalists who have bought into this vision of the future have advised presidents, managed oil empires, and worked as chemists on the Manhattan Project. Even Mussolini was momentarily taken with the reality of biblical prophecy. In the early 1930s, the leader met with two American missionaries, Ralph and Edith Norton, who wanted to interview him for the *Sunday School Times*. Like a lot of fundamentalists of that era, the missionary couple believed Mussolini was a strong candidate for the Antichrist—the dictatorial leader who would resurrect the Roman Empire. As the Nortons quizzed Mussolini about his political intentions and explained the basics of biblical prophecy, Il Duce became fascinated. "Is that really described in the Bible?" he asked. "By the time the Nortons

were through with him," Sutton writes, "Mussolini apparently believed—and maybe even hoped—that he was the long-
awaited world dictator prophesied in the book of Daniel."

During the 1930s the fundamentalist movement more
fully aligned itself with the Republican Party, in response
to the New Deal. Because the Antichrist was believed to be
a totalitarian leader presiding over a one-world government,
believers feared any whiff of federal expansion. (This same fear
produced skepticism toward the United Nations.) The book of
Daniel predicted that end-times government would be "a mix
of iron and clay," which some believers interpreted to mean
totalitarianism brought about through popular democracy. As
President Franklin D. Roosevelt took his turn at regulating
big business and ushered in government programs such as the
Works Progress Administration and Social Security, evangelicals recognized signs of the end. Christian leaders worried that
FDR would, in the words of Keith L. Brooks, "ride roughshod
over the Constitution into the seat of a dictator." William Bell
Riley, the Baptist minister known as "the Grand Old Man of
Fundamentalism," saw in these new programs "the hydra heads
of Socialism and incipient Communism."

While African Americans were largely barred from leadership positions in the fundamentalist movement, black churches
also watched for the coming of Christ—though their signs of
the times had less to do with international politics than with
the injustices taking place on American soil, including lynch-
ing and Jim Crow. (Perhaps the central hypocrisy in the history
of fundamentalist theology is the fact that white evangelicals
managed to find signs of apocalypse in every social evil except
their own prejudice.) At the same time, premillennialism inter-
sected in creative ways with the tradition of black liberation
theology. In 1924 James Webb, a Seattle minister and member

of Marcus Garvey's Universal Negro Improvement Association, claimed, "The universal black king is coming," an allusion to the book of Daniel. This kind of rhetoric would grow in popularity during the 1960s, when black evangelists blended evangelical theology and the Black Power movement to denounce, in apocalyptic terms, the country's legacy of racial injustice. In an ironic twist, evangelicalism, with its rigidly segregated churches and colleges, inspired the moral lexicon of civil rights activists.

Despite such moments of redemption, the story of American premillennialism reads more often like a farce, one in which postexilic Jewish literature is consistently (mis)interpreted in the context of modern geopolitics. Take Gog, an empire described in the book of Ezekiel as an expansive and sinister nation that would sit to the north of Israel. Gog was possibly a reference to ancient Babylon, and yet around the time of the Bolshevik revolution, many believers became convinced that Ezekiel had augured the rise of modern Russia—a symbolism that would persist well into the Cold War; in the words of President Reagan, "What other powerful nation is to the north of Israel? None." During World War II, biblical references to Rome, Gomer, and Magog came to symbolize Mussolini, Hitler, and Stalin, and the merchants of Tarshish in Ezekiel were interpreted as allusions to England. Years later, George W. Bush apparently believed that these empires referred to Iraq and Afghanistan. "Gog and Magog are at work in the Middle East," he told French president Jacques Chirac in a 2003 phone call, appealing to their common Christian faith as a basis for an invasion. "This confrontation is willed by God, who wants to use this conflict to erase His people's enemies before a new age begins." Chirac, a Roman Catholic, promptly asked his staff to call the French Protestant Federation and find out what Bush was talking about.

That Bush and Reagan managed to become leaders of the free world speaks to decades of fundamentalist political ambition. And it's this ambition that is perhaps the most baffling aspect of the movement. One might expect the anticipation of apocalypse would go hand in hand with apathy or social withdrawal. After all, if you believe the world is on the brink of destruction, why bother trying to transform it? But over the years, fundamentalists have become more politically engaged than their liberal Protestant counterparts. Sutton explains this paradox via Christ's parable of the talents. A wealthy man goes on a journey, entrusting each of his servants with a number of talents, a unit of money. When he returns, he assesses what each man has done with their portion—whether they hid it in the ground or invested it—and praises them accordingly. The parable, which is today the vade mecum of the Christian financial planning industry, has long been interpreted in terms of a more expansive brand of stewardship. American believers see themselves as guardians of earthly virtue, charged to "occupy" the Earth until Christ's return.

What is the future of American premillennialism? Or perhaps a better question would be, can this species of fundamentalism be said to have a future? Despite the fact that Sutton's history reveals the adaptability of this theology over the past century, Sutton, in the end, defers to the prevailing view that fundamentalism is on its way out. "Some of the most famous evangelical preachers in the nation no longer talk about a soon-coming apocalypse," he writes in his epilogue. He mentions the emerging church—a new generation of believers who have adopted a postmodern approach to scripture and reject premillennial ideas—and cites Chuck Colson's staid post-9/11 column in *Christianity Today*, in which the preacher wrote, "I try to avoid end-times prophecy."

But this decline in apocalyptic pronouncements doesn't necessarily indicate a shift in doctrine. When Sutton buys it, he, like a lot of secular observers, underestimates how self-aware and media savvy evangelicals have become in the twenty-first century. The public rhetoric of evangelicals—those carefully crafted messages delivered from the pulpit or in print—may not reflect new theological trends so much as the church's public relations acumen. Consider that post-9/11 sobriety. I was a sophomore at Moody Bible Institute when the tragedy occurred. That week our college president, whose chapel address was later broadcast nationally on Moody Radio, delivered a sermon glazed with the language of compassion. He spoke about how to make sense of the senseless, and reminded us that Christ was suffering alongside our nation. But such sermons are less the product of a revised theology than they are the new face of a movement that has come to see tragedies such as 9/11 as media opportunities, occasions to attract unbelievers who've been rattled by seismic horror. Within the privacy of our classrooms, conversations were decidedly more frank. One afternoon my systematic theology professor gave a forty-minute lecture about the perfect alignment between Islamic prophecy and biblical end-times chronology, arguing that Osama bin Laden was the false prophet described in the book of Daniel. Theories of this sort, once unabashedly flaunted by preachers and televangelists, are now increasingly limited to private discussions within the coterie of true believers.

Eager as we may be to relegate such narratives to the dustbin of history, apocalypticism remains a timely subject—and not only because more than 40 percent of Americans believe that Jesus will "definitely" or "probably" return before 2050. The truth is that we live in an era not unlike the one that incubated modern fundamentalism. Like those early twentieth-century Americans who saw progressivism—with its emphasis on rational, technological solutions—as a panacea for social and economic strife, today some of us hope that Silicon Valley visionaries will engineer an earthly utopia. Such visions of the future belie our fears about the present, as climate change and global terror pose increasingly plausible disaster scenarios. Progress and panic have always been two sides of the same coin, and if we dismiss the rants of televangelists, or snicker at the megaphone insanity of street preachers, it is at least in part because they embody an unflattering reflection of our own obsession with apocalypse, because their worldview is the most obvious distillation of the modern death wish. In the end, the history of evangelicalism, cynical and fatalistic as it may be, is very much our own.

2015, *Boston Review*

SNIFFING GLUE

It's 1994, and Michael Stipe recently lost his religion. It's before Bieber and bling, before ordering a latte required six qualifying adjectives. In coffeehouses across the country, bored teens slouch on thrift-store couches nodding along to the Cranberries' "Zombie." Weezer breaks into the alt-rock scene with the Blue Album; Green Day tops the charts with the first punk rock song to whine about a lousy therapist. In April, hordes of fans gather in Seattle Park to mourn the death of Kurt Cobain. A few months later, 350,000 people make the pilgrimage to Saugerties, New York, for the twenty-fifth anniversary of Woodstock.

That September, in Peoria, Illinois, the gospel artist known simply as Carman takes the stage at a sold-out stadium concert. Dressed in a hooded sweatshirt, high-top sneakers, and neon Ray-Bans, he calls out to a crowd of cheering young people: "Who's in the house?"

If you're not familiar with the 1990s contemporary Christian music scene, Carman was kind of a big deal. Born Carmelo Dominic Licciardello in Trenton, New Jersey, Carman began his career as a Las Vegas lounge singer, then got saved and spent much of the '70s and '80s dominating the Christian adult contemporary market. At this concert, he opened with the hit single from his 1993 album *The Standard*, a project designed to court a younger audience.

"Who's in the House" is a hip-hop track about the presence of the Lord. Through megaphone distortion, Carman rapped a few lines: "You take him high / you take him low / you take J.C. wherever you go," then led into a call-and-response hook reminiscent of 1980s-era De La Soul. "Tell me who's in the house? J.C.!"

If you're wondering what teenager in her right mind would listen to a forty-year-old Vegas showman with a Jersey accent rap about Jesus, the answer is: me. In junior high, I saw Carman in concert three times. *The Standard* was the first CD I ever bought. I listened to Carman on my Discman on the way to youth group and dished with my girlfriends about what a hottie he was. At the concerts, I bought his T-shirts and posters, and when he called out "Who's in the house?" I made my arms into letters, "YMCA" style, with the rest of the crowd and shouted "J.C.!"

I was homeschooled up until tenth grade, and my social life revolved around church. I grew up submersed in evangelical youth culture: reading *Brio* magazine, doing devotions in my *Youth Walk* Bible, eagerly awaiting the next installment of the Left Behind series, and developing a taste in music that ran the gamut from Christian rap to Christian pop to Christian rock.

While born-again rockers can be traced back to the Jesus

People movement of the late-1960s and early 1970s, the 1990s was *the* decade of contemporary Christian music, or CCM. In my early teens, new bands were popping up faster than I could follow. And Carman wasn't the only established act revamping his sound for a younger crowd. Jon Gibson, a pop artist who produced what is generally considered the first Christian rap song (1988's "The Wall"), argued that Christian musicians needed to be savvier in presenting teens with the gospel. He told *CCM Magazine*, "I want to sneak into their hearts with the music. Contemporary Christian music needs to branch out a little more, get a little sneakier."

"Meeting kids where they're at" was a relatively new concept for the church. My parents had grown up in an era when teens were supposed to sit in the pew and sing hymns along with everyone else. When I reached middle school, Christian youth leaders were anxiously discussing the battle for "cultural relevance"—one of the many marketing terms adopted by evangelicals. In the '90s, mainline Protestant churches were losing members to the growing evangelical movement. With the explosion of rock concert–style megachurches, many traditional congregations incorporated contemporary worship services in order to attract young people. For our dwindling Baptist congregation, this meant scrapping the organs and old hymns with arcane lyrics like "Now I raise my Ebenezer," and replacing them with praise choruses led by "worship teams" of college kids with guitars and electric violins. It meant sermons full of pop culture allusions, with juicy titles ("Marriage in the Line of Fire," "The Young and the Righteous") designed to make conservative values seem radical and hip.

Traditionally, the church's approach to secular music had been fear tactics: denouncing rock bands, staging record burnings. But this was the golden era of MTV, and Christian leaders, perhaps sensing they were up against a larger beast, opted for a more positive approach by promoting sanctioned (and sanctified) alternatives. Christian concerts became popular youth group events. My friends traveled to blowout festivals with names like Acquire the Fire or Cornerstone. Our youth pastor let us spray-paint the basement teen room with graffiti and tack up posters of born-again acts like Third Day and All Star United. At Wednesday night youth group, in lieu of a message, we'd often watch CCM music videos.

By the time I was finishing up eighth grade, I had ditched my Carman albums and moved on to bands like Audio Adrenaline and Jars of Clay, groups who sported flannel shirts and surfer hair and did songs that sounded like praise choruses transposed into a minor key. "Lift me up—when I am falling / Lift me up—I'm weak and I'm dying." Or the Newsboys, who produced albums like *Hell Is for Wimps* and *Not Ashamed*, and gained popularity for the track "Shine," which assures teens that their faith can appear attractive to nonbelievers:

> *Shine*
> *make them wonder what you've got*
> *make them wish that they were not*
> *on the outside looking bored.*

By far the coolest CCM band when I was a teen was DC Talk. Short for "Decent Christian Talk," this trio of young men from Virginia—one black, two white—started their career as a hip-hop group. They gained popularity with tracks like "Jesus Is Just Alright," which sampled the Doobie Brothers' song and laid down lyrics like:

I'm kicking it Jesus style
To the ones who think they heard
I did use the "J" word
'Cause I ain't too soft to say it
Even if DJs don't play it.

They sang about the decline of Christian morals: "In reality our decency has taken a plunge / 'In God We Trust' is an American pun," and occasionally broke into rhythmic harangues against racism, hypocrisy, or premarital intercourse: "I don't want . . . your sex for now . . . I don't want it till we take the vow." I'm not going to lie: DC Talk was pretty damn good. I might be guilty of still listening to their albums occasionally when no one else is around. Despite the cheesy lyrics, they had a fresh street dance sound—close harmonizing and poppy rap verses. I once played their album *Free at Last* for a friend who hadn't grown up in the church, and he thought it was Color Me Badd.

This, by the way, is considered the ultimate sign of quality CCM, even amongst Christians: the ability to pass as secular. Every band's goal was to have teenagers stop their grooving mid-song and exclaim, like a soda commercial actress who's just realized she's been drinking diet, "Wait, this is *Christian?*" The logic was that the more these bands fit in with what was playing on the radio, the more someone like me would feel comfortable passing their album on to my non-Christian friends (supposing I'd had any), giving them a chance to hear the gospel. Bob Herdman, of the band Audio Adrenaline, argued that his role as a Christian artist was to create music that would seduce kids into a personal encounter with Christ. "You can have fun and discover Christ at the same time," he told the *Orange Country Register* in 1997. "We're just a regular rock band—except we use our God-given gifts to explore our faith and inspire others to do the same." Likewise, the website Metal for Jesus argued that "Christian metal is just as brutal and heavy as the Secular when it comes to the music. What differs is the lyrics." Yes, there's Christian metal. There's even Christian death metal (Living Sacrifice). There's Christian glam rock (Stryper), Christian punk (Relient K), Christian ska (Five Iron Frenzy), Christian techno (World Wide Message Tribe), and Christian industrial (Circle of Dust).

There were still some conservatives who insisted that genres like rock, metal, or rap were so inherently evil that no amount of uplifting lyrics could redeem them. They claimed that beats were hypnotic and certain chord intervals belonged to the devil, and they called attention to the fact that Satan's role, before being kicked out of heaven, was celestial music director. Some quoted scripture like 1 Thessalonians 5:22, which instructs believers to "abstain from all appearance of evil"— not just evil itself, but the accoutrements, like electric guitars and tattoos. But these voices quickly faded into the wilderness. For the most part, believers came to agree with Frank Breeden, president of the Gospel Music Association, who said, "There really is no such thing as a Christian B-flat. Music in itself is an amoral vehicle."

In 1995, DC Talk shocked their fans by releasing *Jesus Freak*, an alt-rock album full of double-tracked power chords and grungy bass lines. It was a dramatically different sound for them. In their album photos, they'd traded in their parachute pants for Carhartts, their Jordans for Chucks. Except for an occasional chanted bridge (the first appearance of rapcore in CCM), they'd abandoned their hip-hop roots. The concept was unlike anything that had been pitched at born-again teens: a celebration of the marginalized believer. The title track alludes to biblical prophets like John the Baptist, portraying them as outcasts:

> *With skins on his back and hair on his face*
> *They thought he was strange by the locusts he ate*
> *The Pharisees tripped when they heard him speak*
> *Until the king took the head off this Jesus freak.*

Band member Toby McKeehan explained that the idea was to reclaim the term "Jesus freak." "It was a negative phrase back in the late sixties and early seventies," he said. "If you were a 'Jesus Freak,' that was people talking down to you. We've chosen to take the opposite approach and say that that's something to be happy about."

It's worth pointing out that this was around the time Beck was singing "I'm a loser, baby," and Thom Yorke was droning "I'm a creep." If I had flipped through FM radio that summer, I might have heard The Offspring ("I'm just a sucker with no self-esteem"), or Green Day ("Sometimes I give myself the creeps"), or Gwen Stefani ("Guess I'm some kind of freak"). The irony is that DC Talk's album, for all its glorification of ostracized misfits, was the most culturally relevant CCM album of the decade. The title song impeccably mirrored that "Yeah, I'm a loser, so what?" attitude: "I don't really care if they label me a Jesus Freak." The concept was pretty brilliant. My friends and I were getting to the age where we were beginning to sense that being a believer wasn't exactly cool. Being a born-again could get you called a goody-goody, a narc, or a tight-ass. Being a Jesus freak, on the other hand, seemed kind of okay—edgy, authentic, and biblically sound.

The international Freak Show tour came through Peoria that

summer, and I attended it with my friend Jenna, both our little sisters, plus her mom as chaperone at the packed Peoria Civic Center. Much to my relief, we didn't stand out: most of the kids there were our age—preteens, many of them girls, towing frazzled adults in their wake. There was a mosh pit; there was crowd surfing. There was also a presentation of the gospel and an altar call. Toward the end, DC Talk did an acoustic set, complete with an unfurled Turkish rug and candelabras just like *MTV Unplugged.* Then they amped up again, for a high-voltage cover of "Purple Haze" and left the stage, only to be goaded back for an encore. (CCM concerts often included secular covers. DC Talk sometimes closed with Nirvana's "All Apologies"—except instead of singing the line "everyone is gay," they changed it to "Jesus is the way." I'm not making this up.) We left the stadium ecstatic. Riding home, we four girls sat in the back of the minivan headbanging to the CD, which we'd asked Jenna's mom to please play at full volume.

Jesus Freak went double platinum and won a Grammy for Best Rock Gospel Album. It climbed to number sixteen on the Billboard 200 and led to appearances on Jay Leno and Arsenio Hall. DC Talk produced a gritty music video for "Jesus Freak," which was spliced with black-and-white newsreel footage of race riots and World War II propaganda films. *Billboard* claimed that "the clip's slick style and in your face imagery could easily fit between cutting edge videos from the likes of Nirvana and Nine Inch Nails." DC Talk told the magazine that the intention of the clip was to "push the envelope" of the Christian music community and reach a wider audience.

Some Christian critics accused them of trying to cross over. It was the height of the grunge era, a convenient time to hop on the rock bandwagon. But DC Talk repeatedly resisted making the switch, unlike U2, a band to whom they were often compared (and whom Christians disowned around the late '80s, when Adam Clayton got arrested for possession). The reason that DC Talk never gained mainstream appeal is they refused to tone down their gospel message. As McKeehan put it, "Music is our tool. Our message is Christ." Like most CCM artists of that era, they saw themselves primarily as evangelists. One reviewer noted the same about Carman: "He doesn't make music for the sake of music, or artistry. He makes music as an evangelism tool. Indeed, Carman is more like a singing evangelist than a singer." This was the reason Christian rock had a reputation for being shoddy, and it was also the reason that so many Christian artists switched genres—not just evolved but completely changed their sound and look and ethos. The music was always a vehicle for the message, and if artists believed there was a more effective way to reach kids with that message, by all means they'd do it. DC Talk simply had a more ambitious ministry than anyone else in the game. When asked about the impetus behind *Jesus Freak*, band member Michael Tait said, "We wanted to write songs that would hopefully touch a generation."

I saw MTV for the first time when I was thirteen. My parents, like most of my friends' parents, didn't have cable, and I literally had to go halfway around the world to see it. In November of 1995, my grandfather went on a trip to Moscow and took my sister Sheena and me along. He was on the board of an organization that was lobbying to teach "Christian ethics" in Russian schools. It was supposed to be an educational experience, but we hardly left the hotel. All week, he attended back-to-back meetings while Sheena and I stayed in our room, eating duty-free chocolate and gorging ourselves on MTV Europe.

On one of those gray afternoons I saw Nirvana's "Smells Like

Teen Spirit" video. In a smoky warehouse, the band and a team of tattooed cheerleaders performed for bleachers full of kids. As the song progresses, the scene dissolves into anarchy: the students jump off the bleachers, strip off their clothes, destroy the band's equipment, and light the entire set on fire. I watched this perched on the edge of my bed, about three feet from the TV screen, while Sheena was taking a nap. I didn't catch any of the lyrics, but I was mesmerized by Kurt Cobain stumbling around the set, squinting into the light, barely suppressing a sneer. I couldn't have told you what the word "irony" meant, but I knew I'd been cheated by Christian rock. This was crack, and I'd been wasting my time sniffing glue.

In the mid-1990s, MTV was producing a product superior to just about anything pitched at teens, largely due to its revolutionary market research. The Brand Strategy and Planning division of MTV was a new department dedicated to researching kids in the channel's target demographic (ages twelve to twenty-four). They conducted hundreds of in-depth ethnography studies, where researchers would visit a typical fan—say a sixteen-year-old girl—in her home. Armed with a clipboard and trailed by a camera crew, these researchers would hang out in the fan's room and listen to her talk about her favorite pair of shoes, or what's in her CD player, or her relationship with her boyfriend.

The department also conducted focus groups that brought together teens who had been identified as "leading-edge thinkers and tastemakers and stylemakers" in eighteen American cities. Another study polled three hundred kids from up-and-coming neighborhoods of New York and Los Angeles to find out what they were listening to. Additional research was contracted to "cool-hunting" companies like Youth Intelligence that had hundreds of field correspondents snapping photos of street fashion, getting down in mosh pits, chatting up kids outside bars, and collecting similar information that was compiled and sorted into a web database to which MTV—along with other clients—subscribed for an annual six-figure fee. "It's principally to make our programming relevant," Todd Cunningham, senior vice president of brand strategy and planning at MTV, said in a 1995 interview. By comparison, the CCM market of this era seems tragically naïve. Christian bands could mimic what was already mainstream, but it was difficult to compete with a product created with the help of millions of dollars' worth of demographic research. Cultural relevance could be bought, and MTV, part of media conglomerate Viacom, had a very large budget.

That trip to Russia was a conversion experience. The images I watched on TV were more vivid than anything I saw from the charter bus window. The Smashing Pumpkins were on rotation then, especially "1979" with the suburban kids knocking over liquor-store shelves, giving the finger to their town from the top of a hill. There was Garbage's "Stupid Girl," fronted by Shirley Manson with her combat boots and sexy nihilism, and Metallica's "Until It Sleeps," a tableau of grotesque religious iconography. I stayed up late watching the same videos over and over.

I spent the following years obsessively listening to the radio and befriending the youth group kids whose parents didn't child block MTV. I wrote down the names of bands I didn't know, then biked to the local record store, Believe in Music, and spent my babysitting money on albums I had to smuggle back to my room. With very few exceptions (Disney soundtracks) my parents didn't let me listen to secular music, but there were a few bands I managed to pass off as Christian, like Soul Asylum or Collective Soul. It was an easy feat at the time: Christian rock was becoming more sophisticated, and the secular industry was oddly fascinated with God. Artists on heavy rotation on MTV included Joan Osborne: "If God had a name, what would it be? And would you call it to his face?" Alanis Morissette: "I am fascinated by the spiritual man," Counting Crows: "Says she's close to understanding Jesus," and Tori Amos: "I've been looking for a savior in these dirty streets."

This wasn't coincidental. One of the "macro trends" MTV uncovered in their research was a growing interest in spirituality among teens. "Trendsetters," the study argued, "feel as if music today has no depth, no meaning. . . . They are looking for meaning from their music and music that expresses their search for meaning." The Music Trendsetters Study coined the word "pessimysticism," an attitude that expresses "a simultaneous dissatisfaction with the inauthenticity of commercial music, and a search for higher emotion and expression in music." For most of my high school years, I noticed an odd disconnect: everyone at church was bemoaning the fact that kids were no longer interested in spirituality, and yet all I heard on MTV was stuff about God. As CCM strove to keep up with an industry teens resented for its spiritual vacuity, MTV reached the acme of its marketing genius: its ability to take its audience's disenchantment with commercialism, repackage it, and sell it back to them.

I listened to "Smells Like Teen Spirit" dozens of times during those years, yet I never caught on to the words. Cobain slurred his words, and the liner notes to *Nevermind* didn't include lyrics. It wasn't until I was in college, listening to the track on campus radio, that I realized the song was a taunt—a wry dare to an industry that panders to young consumers: "I feel stupid and contagious / Here we are now, entertain us." It expresses the rage of teens who have been asked for nothing more than their passive, profitable attention—and their cynical awareness that this rage will inevitably be aired on a media conglomerate network, between commercials for deodorant. I didn't catch all of that at thirteen; all I knew was that this music made me stop feeling like a sheltered and naïve homeschooler. I knew it made me smarter and hipper than the kids at church—that it made me less of a sucker in a world that was trying, on all fronts, to dupe me.

Few evangelical teens today are probably familiar with the name Fanny Crosby, but if you were to open a Christian hymnal, you would see her name on dozens of the choruses. Before praise and worship bands took over, our church sang her hymns like "Blessed Assurance" and "He Hideth My Soul" in our Sunday services. Crosby—a blind rescue mission worker during the Civil War—is considered the "Queen of Gospel Songwriters," but before she became a Christian, she wrote popular songs. Her most famous tune, "Rosalie, the Prairie Flower," earned her nearly three thousand dollars in royalties—a staggering amount in her day. Once she began writing hymns, she claimed that she sometimes had to reject the melodies musicians proposed because they sounded too close to the secular tunes that were currently in fashion. She believed in an ideal that today seems ridiculous in all but the most fundamentalist circles: that Christian culture should remain set apart from the trends and caprices of the world. She feared that in using familiar tunes, people "would think that Fanny Crosby who once wrote for the people in the saloons has merely changed the lyrics."

By the early 2000s, straddling the spiritual-secular line was precisely the goal of CCM groups. Popular bands like Creed,

Switchfoot, and Lifehouse specialized in songs with vaguely romantic, vaguely spiritual lyrics, so they could be picked up by both Christian and secular markets. Jars of Clay, whose 1995 debut contained explicitly spiritual content, had lightened up considerably by the release of 2002's *The Eleventh Hour*. In a review of the album, NPR's Scott Simon wrote, "to the uninitiated, many of the tunes could be taken for straight-ahead, modern-pop love songs . . . their subject could be God or a girl." Guitarist Matt Odmark admits they made a conscious effort, in the project, to avoid "the noisy vocabulary of religion."

Lifehouse's "Hanging by a Moment"—which was the number one single of 2001—is a more well-known example of this trend:

> *Desperate for changing,*
> *starving for truth*
> *I'm closer to where I started,*
> *I'm chasing after you.*

Although singer/songwriter Jason Wade identified as a Christian and was embraced by the CCM market—his band met playing in a worship team at church—he claimed that Lifehouse was not a "Christian" band. In an interview with *Rolling Stone*, he said, "We don't want to be labeled as a 'Christian band,' because all of a sudden people's walls come up, and they won't listen to your music and what you have to say."

Basically, CCM caught on to the number one rule of coolness: don't let your marketing show. The best bands—the successful ones, at least—learned to gloss over the gospel message the same way TV producers camouflaged corporate sponsorship. Explicitly Christian lyrics prevented DC Talk from crossing over to the secular market in the '90s; today it's difficult to imagine their unapologetic faith making it in the Christian circuit.

This trend spreads beyond CCM into many areas of evangelical culture. The church is becoming increasingly consumer friendly. Jacob Hill, director of "worship arts" at New Walk Church, describes the Sunday service music as "exciting, loud, powerful, and relevant," and boasts that "a lot of people say they feel like they've just been at a rock concert." Over the past ten years, I've visited churches that have Starbucks kiosks in the foyer and youth wings decked out with air hockey tables. I've witnessed a preacher stop his sermon to play a five-minute clip from *Billy Madison*. I've walked into a sanctuary that was blasting the Black Eyed Peas' "Let's Get It Started" to get the congregation pumped for the morning's message, which was on joy. I have heard a *pastor* say, from a *pulpit*, "Hey, I'm not here to preach at anyone." And yet, in spite of these efforts, churches are retaining only 4 percent of the young people raised in their congregations.

Despite all the affected teenage rebellion, I continued to call myself a Christian into my early twenties. When I finally stopped, it wasn't because being a believer made me uncool or outdated or freakish. It was because being a Christian no longer meant anything. It was a label to slap on my Facebook page, next to my music preferences. The gospel became just another product someone was trying to sell me, and a paltry one at that, because the church isn't Viacom: it doesn't have a Department of Brand Strategy and Planning. Staying relevant in late consumer capitalism requires highly sophisticated resources and the willingness to tailor your values to whatever your audience wants. In trying to compete in this market, the church has forfeited the one advantage it had in the game to attract disillusioned youth: authenticity. When it comes to intransigent values, the profit-driven world has zilch to offer. If Christian leaders weren't so ashamed of those unvarnished values, they might have something more attractive than anything on today's bleak moral market. In the meantime, they've lost one more kid to the competition.

2011, *Guernica*

AMERICAN NICENESS

Upon hearing that someone had published a lengthy study of American niceness, undoubtedly the work of years, my first impulse was to pity her unfortunate timing. Of all the things our era may eventually connote, it seems fair to assume that niceness will not be one of them. But then, have Americans ever been nice? Already it is difficult to remember the not-so-distant past, but the most familiar epithets would seem to suggest otherwise: the Ugly American, the Loud American, the Vulgar American.

According to Carrie Tirado Bramen, the author of *American Niceness: A Cultural History*, these archetypes are intimately bound up with the idea of niceness. The American character is defined by a kind of doubleness, she argues, with niceness and nastiness being two sides of the same coin. If the Old World aspired to civility, a rigid code that moderated social interactions between the classes, the New World went for niceness, a cruder virtue. Rather than cultivating the self-discipline to avoid stomping on toes in the first place, the nice American assumes a spirit of cheery sociability to compensate for a host of transgressions. Bramen acknowledges that the very idea of a national affect may seem quaint, perhaps even regressive, recalling the catalogue of dusty national archetypes—the efficient German, the lazy Irishman—that began as xenophobic specters and somehow persist even in an era of accelerated globalization. But she's interested in how this temperament has been constructed as a sociopolitical device across the past two and a half centuries.

American Niceness was inspired, in part, by the aftermath of 9/11, when the question "Why do they hate us?" became such a popular refrain that George W. Bush included it in his speech to Congress weeks after the attack. For Bramen, the question was another way of asking "Why don't they like us?" It obscured the history of American interventionist tactics in the Middle East by making the tragedy into "a failure of likability." At the root of this query, Bramen locates a willful innocence, a national ethos that refuses to acknowledge its own capacity for violence. "Niceness implies that Americans are fundamentally well-meaning people defined by an essential goodness," she writes. "Even acts of aggression are framed as passive, reluctant, and defensive acts to protect oneself against the potential aggression of another." At this point, my pity for the book's seemingly ill-timed publication vanished—its immediate relevance was obvious. "Well, I think I'm a nice person. I really do," Donald Trump said, in 2015, on *Meet the Press*. He added, "When I made, you know, harsh statements about various people, that was always in response to their criticism of me."

Bramen traces this impulse back to our nation's origins,

when the passive framing of the Declaration of Independence
("it becomes necessary") presented the Revolution as a grudg-
ing act of war instigated by British tyranny. But niceness came
into full fruition, she argues, in the nineteenth century, her
area of scholarly expertise. This was the period when America
became an imperial power, and Bramen demonstrates the ways
in which niceness served as a cheery façade pasted over violence
and injustice. The culture of "Southern hospitality" perpetu-
ated the belief that American slavery was a kinder, more com-
passionate variety than that practiced in the Caribbean. Later in
the century, the annexation of the Philippines was heralded as
a mission of "benevolent assimilation," a phrase that President
William McKinley used in his 1898 speech to the occupied
nation to suggest that, unlike the Spanish Empire, Americans
would be nice. "We come not as invaders or conquerors, but as
friends," McKinley proclaimed. Bramen also examines feminine niceness in the novels of Louisa May Alcott and Harriet
Beecher Stowe ("a major theorist of American niceness"), and
in female-led city missions like Jane Addams's Hull House.
During an era of exploitive industrialism and urban alienation,
women were often encouraged to take on acts of "neighborli-
ness," reflecting the assumption that "interpersonal amiability
can placate class tensions."

It would be easy, of course, to dismiss niceness with wholesale cynicism. Any nation that lays claim to certain principles,
just like any person who dares to do so, opens itself up to the
charge of hypocrisy. But some of the best moments in Bramen's
history ask what might happen were we to actually live up to
our ideals. Appeals to niceness, she notes, have fostered ethical
practices and brought attention to human rights abuses. Bramen cites John Augustus Stone's 1829 play, *Metamora*, which
dramatized Native American hospitality for white audiences in

order to portray the genocide of indigenous peoples as a tragedy of niceness betrayed. Reviews of the play suggest that it
helped at least a few Jackson-era Americans come to terms with
national guilt.

Such narratives point to what Bramen calls a "counter-
tradition" of niceness, "one that linked a shame-based model
of moral outrage with a call for national humility." Still, she
remains skeptical that such gestures can have a lasting effect. If
niceness allows us to reckon, on occasion, with legacies of violence, these gestures just as often become merely therapeutic,
another avenue to catharsis and forgetting. A sunny spirit of
inclusion can obscure structural inequities, and the rehearsal
of clichés and truisms—even those meant to acknowledge past
errors—can reinforce the illusion of our own blamelessness and
ease the conscience into a kind of historical amnesia. The political scientist Michael Rogin has dubbed this process "motivated
forgetting."

I live in Wisconsin, a place where niceness is so ubiquitous that
it seems practically constitutional, so it may be unsurprising
that I found Bramen's thesis convincing, and a little unsettling.
Congeniality has always come easily to me, almost by default;
my husband claims that he frequently wakes to me murmur-
ing litanies of consolation—"No worries, no worries"—in my
sleep. Perhaps for this reason, I've long suspected it to be a substitute for more demanding virtues. In this part of the country,
niceness is less an expression of generosity than it is of reserve:
assuming an inoffensive blandness is a way to avoid drawing
attention to oneself, and the most reliable means of keeping
others at bay. I recall reading, with a pang of recognition, Lorrie Moore's observation, in her short story "Childcare," that the

phrase "sounds good" functions for midwestern girls as a kind of exit strategy. "It was the Midwestern girl's reply to everything," the narrator reflects. "It appeared to clinch a deal . . . except that it was promiseless—mere affirmative description. It got you away, out the door."

This regional variety of niceness can also carry more hostile undertones. In 2015, Mike Pence, who was then the governor of Indiana, defended his state's Religious Freedom Restoration Act against charges that it would allow businesses to discriminate on the basis of a person's sexual identity. On an episode of *This Week with George Stephanopoulos*, Pence, with an air of exasperation, said, "Hoosiers don't believe in discrimination. . . . Anybody that's been in Indiana for five minutes knows that Hoosier hospitality is not a slogan, it's a reality. People tell me, when I travel around the country, 'Gosh, I went to your state and people are so nice.'"

I suspect that fewer Americans now regard niceness as aspirational than did in the past. Most of my fellow millennials would likely prefer to be known as fierce, unapologetic. But the posture of innocence remains seductive. More than once while reading Bramen, I was reminded of the characters in Greg Jackson's stories, thirtysomethings of the creative class who are acutely aware of their comfortable status in a nation known for its decadence and waste, who nevertheless need to assure themselves of their inherent goodness by driving Priuses and donating to charity and returning, via hallucinogens, to a state of childlike credulity. "We thought we were not bad people," observes the narrator of "Wagner in the Desert." "Not the best, a bit spoiled, maybe, but pleasant, insouciantly decent." An apparent article of faith among young Americans on the left, a group in which I include myself, is that while we may belong to an ugly nation, we ourselves constitute a more benign and welcoming elect, a distinction that seems to depend less on the civic duties we have undertaken or the sacrifices we have made than it does on the fact that we use the right pronouns and ritually acknowledge our privilege and buy fair trade.

Niceness, Bramen notes, is a virtue of "surfaces rather than depths." Of all the qualities that might constitute a national character, it is surely the most passive, the closest to sheer indifference. Kindness requires active engagement. Compassion involves some measure of vulnerability. But niceness demands so little. It allows you to turn your back and slip out the door, grabbing your coat and calling out, over your shoulder, those sweet and empty wishes that facilitate so many exits: Sounds good. Take care. Have a nice day.

2017, *The New Yorker*

MATERNAL ECSTASIES

According to the literary critic Lytton Strachey, Florence Nightingale was consumed by an unnatural spirit. "A demon possessed her," he wrote in his 1918 biographical essay on the Englishwoman who pioneered modern nursing. "It was not by gentle sweetness and womanly self-abnegation that she had brought order out of chaos in the Scutari hospitals," he wrote. "It was by strict method, by stern disciplines, by rigid attention to detail, by ceaseless labour, by the fixed determination of an indomitable will." Strachey aimed to dethrone the angelic "lady with the lamp" who lived in the popular imagination, a reputation he believed was idealized and overblown, and in doing so, conjured another caricature, a precursor to Ken Kesey's Nurse Ratched. The Nightingale of Strachey's account was autocratic and severe, methodical to the point of inflexibility. After long days of imposing her meticulous regulations on disorderly hospitals, she would stay up late into the night pouring her "pent up" energies into vitriolic letters addressed to her subordinates. This perverse disposition, the critic concluded, arose because Nightingale had refused the "inevitable habiliments of a Victorian marriage" and the domestic life it would have entailed. Her "possession," then, stemmed from an absence. She was haunted by a nurturing instinct gone haywire, having suppressed "the most powerful and the profoundest of all the instincts of humanity": marriage and motherhood.

Nightingale's own writings reveal a mind more humane and complex. She believed she had been called by God to a solitary life and often spoke of her work as a spiritual vocation. She feared, more than anything, the breach of autonomy that befell Victorian mothers. "Women never have a half-hour . . . that they can call their own," she wrote in her diary at the age of thirty-two, an idea that inspired Virginia Woolf, several decades later, to write *A Room of One's Own*. And yet Strachey was not alone in his diagnosis; Nightingale's early biographers were convinced that she was afflicted with neurasthenia, a nervous disorder thought to derive from overexertion, which one medical journal referred to as "Nature's protest against the childless condition." Her sickness—likely a case of brucellosis contracted in the Crimea—was believed to be the consequence of resisting the transformative, and presumably relaxing, power of motherhood.

The heroine of Emma Donoghue's new novel *The Wonder* is an English nurse in her late twenties who trained under Nightingale and served with her at Scutari during the Crimean War. Like Nightingale, Lib Wright is a single woman who comes from an upper-middle-class family. "My father was a gentleman," Lib tells a doctor upon arriving at her new job in rural Ireland, then immediately feels ashamed for distinguishing herself by her class. In fact, Nightingale's reforms would transform nursing, long regarded as a dirty form of menial labor for the lower classes, into a respectable occupation for educated women.

Several years after her work with Nightingale, Lib is summoned to central Ireland to supervise Anna O'Donnell, an eleven-year-old who claims she has been living for months without food, subsisting only on immaterial "manna from heaven." Religious tourists have made pilgrimages from around the world to pay homage, and the girl's own family believes she is a saint. A local commission, headed by the family's doctor, has decided that Anna must be carefully observed to determine whether she is eating in secret. For several hours each day, Lib sits vigil in the girl's room and takes notes on her behavior, watchful for any suspicious activity.

Lib, it turns out, is ideally suited for the task. Skeptical of the girl's miraculous powers, she quickly becomes obsessed with exposing her—though she cannot decide whether the girl is running the sham alone, or in collusion with her family. Mentally she refers to the girl as "the little fraud," and to her father as "the grand showman behind the scenes." Though a nominal member of the Church of England, Lib is effectively an atheist, a modern woman who believes in nothing more transcendent than the scientific method. To her, rural Ireland is an ignorant backwater littered with obscure Catholic sacraments and the pagan superstitions that preceded them. She shudders at the mystical rituals of the O'Donnell house—putting charms on the butter, setting out saucers of milk to keep away the fairies—unable to fathom the credulity of her hosts. "Is there nothing the Irish won't swallow?" she asks herself.

Ireland in the 1850s was a land of poverty and disease, still reeling from the potato famine of the previous decade. The novel, much to its credit, eludes the visions of cozy Éire that live so quaintly in the North American imagination in favor of something closer to a historical reality—particularly as it might be seen through the prejudices of a well-off English-woman (Lib describes the country as "one endless, waterlogged mire"). Donoghue was born in Ireland and lived there until she was twenty, and she deftly re-creates the country's historical landscape. The book is impressively textured with the breadth of her voluminous research. She knows, for instance, that residents of thatch-roofed houses were obliged to keep a fire going even during the heat of the summer to keep the roof dry and preserve the timbers; and that a Grub Street journalist would not compare a fasting eleven-year-old girl to a mere "circus freak," but rather a "Feejee mermaid at a raree-show."

Though Donoghue is a prolific and longtime author of historical fiction, she has become best known for a project that diverged from her larger body of work—the contemporary novel *Room*, which tells the story of a sexual prisoner confined with her five-year-old son to a garden shed with only a television and a collection of homemade toys to entertain them. Despite the sensationalist premise, the novel can be read as a rather moving metaphor for the isolating experience of modern motherhood. (The book sold more than two million copies and is now a major motion picture that earned Brie Larson Best Actress at the 2016 Oscars.)

Like *Room*, *The Wonder* is also about motherhood, though it approaches the subject from a more oblique angle. At the beginning of the novel, Lib is as skeptical of familial love as she is of the fairies. In fact, it disgusts her. Whenever Anna's mother embraces her daughter, the nurse can hardly tolerate the display of affection. She feels it is "something out of grand opera, the way she [barges] in to make a show of her maternal feelings twice a day," and "the whole performance [sets]

Lib's teeth on edge." She maintains a safe—which is to say scientific—distance from Anna, keeping watch from a straight-backed chair and carefully logging the child's daily intake, which consists solely of teaspoons of water.

Devotional fasting might seem an odd novelistic subject in an age when such inclinations, especially in adolescent girls, are regarded as more clinical than spiritual. But Anna displays none of the obsessive behaviors characteristic of girls with eating disorders. The child passes her days serenely reading scripture and whispering prayers. She is quick-witted and laughs easily, and seems—at least at first—to have genuinely transcended her need for food. Curiously, it is Lib who displays the hypervigilance so common in anorexics. She keeps obsessive notes throughout the day and regards her own eating and sleeping habits with a kind of monomaniacal precision. If the pair were transported to a contemporary landscape, it would be the nurse, not the adolescent, keeping a food journal and wearing a digital bracelet to tally calories.

To be sure, the English nurse's presence in this tiny Irish hamlet foreshadows the inevitable global triumph of the modern over the ancient, of systemized Protestant efficiency overtaking the drafty world of Catholic superstition. Lib changes Anna's sheets each day like clockwork, measures the girl's walks with the punctiliousness of a railroad conductor, and checks off each performed duty in her notebook with the exactitude she learned from Nightingale in the Crimea. Nightingale herself appears sporadically throughout the novel, in flashbacks. Donoghue's version of the historical figure—Miss N., as Lib calls her—seems to owe no small debt to Strachey's biography. She stands as a parody of ironclad proceduralism, a woman whose contact with the world of men and science has irreparably damaged her nurturing instinct. "Miss N. warned against personal affection as much as she did against romance," Lib recalls. "Lib had been taught to watch for attachments in any form and root them out." When a fellow nurse at Scutari complained that they weren't allowed to follow "*the prompts of the heart*—to take a quarter of an hour, for instance, to sit with a dying man and offer words of comfort," Nightingale replied with a coldhearted appeal to efficiency: "Don't listen to your heart, listen to me and get on with your work."

There's a marked hostility toward scientific expertise quickening beneath the pages of this story. In these moments the novel, despite its firm historical grounding, feels eerily modern. A similar skepticism animated *Room*—particularly in its latter half, where both the medical establishment and the media are regarded as intrusions into the domestic sanctum, the inscrutable world of mother and child. "Families all [have] their peculiar ways that [can't] be discerned by outsiders," Lib observes of the O'Donnells in a rare moment of generosity. It's a sentiment Donoghue has also put forth in her nonfiction, one that undoubtedly appeals to mothers exhausted by the slew of authoritative yet conflicting prescriptions about immunization schedules, breastfeeding, and the like. The novel seems to be slyly advancing a case for the authority of maternal instinct over institutional logic, a defense of the sort of knowledge that arises intuitively. Reformers like Lib and Nightingale might have all the book knowledge at their disposal, but they don't "get it" because they're not mothers.

The Wonder is ultimately a story of transformation—the tale of a woman passing from one side of this divide to the other. Despite herself, Lib begins to enjoy her shifts with Anna. Walking with the child along the green and spongy bog, "the soft skin of Ireland," Lib too becomes supple, and as the child's health begins to fail she finds herself increasingly invested in her survival. As is often the case with awakenings, she hardly notices the changes taking place within her until someone else points them out. When she finally implores the doctor who hired her to consider force-feeding Anna, the physician attributes the breach of professionalism—a nurse advising her superior—to the fact that the child has stimulated Lib's "dormant maternal capacity."

Soon, Lib dispenses with her note-taking and finds herself resorting to maternal desperation. Despite her professed atheism, she begins praying for Anna's life to be spared. "Lib [sees] the point of such superstition" for the first time: "If there was a ritual she could perform that offered a chance of saving Anna, wouldn't she try it? She'd bow down to a tree or a rock or a carved turnip for the child's sake." When she decides to take drastic—and markedly unprofessional—action to save Anna's life, her transformation is complete: "For the first time, Lib understood the wolfishness of mothers." Suffice to say that Lib does become a mother by the end of the book, though she comes by it in a roundabout way.

Donoghue has presided for some years now over a literary empire that envisions motherhood as a kind of religion, and *The Wonder* stands as an unmistakable conversion narrative. It is the story of a woman denying, resisting, and ultimately accepting the call to nurture. Even within the context of Donoghue's previous work, *The Wonder* is especially insistent—at times even polemical—on the nourishing effects of childbearing. *Room* dramatized motherhood as an essentially ascetic vocation: its heroine had been chosen in a unique capacity and hermetically sealed away from the world, hence the saintly imagery that populated that novel and the frequent evocations of its protagonist and her son as Mary and the baby Jesus. But in *The*

Wonder, motherhood is a universal vocation. It is a spiritual calling, one that, like Luther's notion of salvation, is granted to all in equal measure and must nevertheless be discovered through personal awakening. Women who spurn the maternal impulse, the book suggests, are suppressing the power of the spirit within them, as unnatural as a young girl quashing her God-given hunger. In the end, the book makes explicit the inversion that was implied from the beginning: Lib is actually the one refusing sustenance by denying herself the gratification of familial love. "To fast was to hold fast to emptiness, to say no and no and no again," she observes, near the end of the book. While the story itself is coy about the implications of this inversion, it's tempting to read into Donoghue's vast ecology of metaphors a troublesome import: that childlessness is a kind of starvation, a willful spiritual emptiness.

This drama of resistance and surrender feels similarly of our time. Lib's transformation is very much in tune with contemporary memoirists like Sarah Manguso and Rachel Cusk, who've come reluctantly to motherhood and borne witness to their own bewildered conversions. "I never wanted to be a mother," Manguso writes in an essay for *Harper's* titled "The Grand Shattering." "I now look back at my old life, when I believed myself to be as happy and fulfilled as a person could be, with the same maternal pity I used to despise." Motherhood, she writes, is "a shattering, a disintegration of the self, after which the original form is quite gone." Even Cusk, who doesn't find motherhood particularly miraculous, is adamant about its irrevocable alterations to the self. "To be a mother I must leave the telephone unanswered, work undone, arrangements unmet," she writes in her memoir *A Life's Work*. "To be myself I must let the baby cry, must forestall her hunger or leave her for evenings out, must forget her in order to think about other things. To succeed in being one means to fail at being the other." Motherhood, we are so often told, is sweeping in its powers of transfiguration. It can make a woman more empathetic, more emotionally acute, more attuned to the injustices of the world. If one is to believe the rhetoric at this year's Democratic National Convention, it can even make her a better president.

It is difficult in these days of wild and consuming transformation (and here, alas, I am speaking from experience) for the childless woman not to feel a bit like the reprobate stubbornly occupying the back pew, refusing salvation. Or like an anorexic, declining the nutrients that will sustain her. "Why am I starving, desperate, diseased upon it?" Nightingale wrote in her diary in one of her darker moments. It's a sentiment that remains, a century and a half later, dismayingly easy to recognize.

Has motherhood always demanded such dramatic metamorphoses? Has it ever inspired such furies of doubt? It was not so long ago that Betty Friedan argued that feminism was built on the realization that women "couldn't live . . . in terms of motherhood alone." The promise of that foundational second wave was that a woman's identity needn't be consumed by the crèche, that she could have children without being wholly defined by her capacity to nurture. Of course, Friedan and her allies came of age in an era when motherhood was still understood as an essentially catholic undertaking, a destiny into which women were born and that rested on a tradition of unquestioned sacraments and collective expectations. Just as the Reformation introduced the necessity of personal transformation, it's perhaps inevitable that motherhood, too—as the cultural imperatives for its existence have dwindled—has come to assume an aspect of *sola fide*, a faith that cannot be simply performed but felt, and must be justified constantly in every facet of one's life. To become a mother, we are told, a woman must surrender everything, spirit and flesh. But most crucially, she must come to *believe*—in the importance of the task, and in her capacity to become a new being.

2016, *The Los Angeles Review of Books*

PURE MICHIGAN

If you live anywhere along the wide swath of the Rust Belt, you've probably seen the television spots. There are a dozen or so variants, but each ad begins in the same manner, with cinematic piano music and sweeping, aerial shots of lighthouses and crashing waves. They show beaches of unblemished Kalkaska sand and kids cannonballing off floating docks. The narration is reminiscent of the copy found in certain resort brochures in that it seeks not merely to describe the locale but to evoke an entire experience: "The perfect summer has a voice . . ." begins one. "It whispers one more game, one more swim, one more round." The ads are paid for by Travel Michigan, a division of the state's economic development corporation, and end, always, with the tagline "Pure Michigan."

About a year ago, my husband and I, who have spent most of our adult lives in the major cities of the Midwest, moved to

Muskegon, a small town on the western coast of the lower peninsula. The ads, which air regularly in Milwaukee, Cincinnati, Indianapolis, and Chicago, air here too. I suppose they're trying to reach people who are passing through. Or maybe the ads are meant for us, the residents, as a morale boost of sorts, a reminder that life here is good. Muskegon is an old lumber town whose economic telos ended the day Chicago discovered steel, but it has persisted through several recessions and decades of industrial decline. I grew up here, and my husband and I moved back to be closer to family, though I suppose we were also drawn by the prospect of clean air and solitude, of freshwater swims along the eerie, Galapagos-like stillness of deserted beaches. On some mornings in early summer, the shallows along the shoreline are like glass, the water so clear it looks chlorinated.

While the Pure Michigan ads pay homage to places all over the state, a great deal of the footage features the western shoreline of Lake Michigan, from St. Joseph all the way to the Upper Peninsula. There are shots of canoes traversing the oceanic blue coastline along Sleeping Bear Dunes and of anglers roll-casting in shaded tributaries. The ads clearly convey that this is a place of water, and that the water is, as the tagline suggests, pure. "Water," a deep male voice intones. "We take our showers with it, we make our coffee with it, but we rarely tap its true potential and just let it be itself, flowing freely into clean lakes, clear streams, and along more freshwater coastline than any other state in the country." It's not impossible to imagine the voice, coupled with aerial shots, as belonging to God himself.

In fact, it belongs to the actor Tim Allen, a Michigan native whose longtime role as Tim "the Toolman" Taylor established him as the quintessential father figure of Middle America, and whose warm baritone has lent the ads what *Forbes* magazine called a "'mystical' power." (I suspect the effect only lands for some—my younger sister hears Buzz Lightyear.) The piano music is likewise lifted from the movies, from the sound track of the 1999 film *The Cider House Rules*. The song evokes the kind of autumnal sentimentalism that animates Starbucks ads and late-career Diane Keaton films.

The ads, which are now entering their tenth year, have proved the most successful tourism campaign in the state's history. Every buck spent on the Pure Michigan ads has returned to the state almost seven dollars in tourism revenue, and the record number of visitors in 2014 was widely trumpeted as the fruit of the campaign. There are now Pure Michigan coasters, sweatshirts, tee tags, and boat bags. You can get a custom license plate emblazoned with the slogan. On Facebook and Instagram, users post photos of sunsets and buckets of ripe apples appended with the hashtag #puremichigan. The campaign has, in other words, radically transcended its initial effort to entice visitors to the state and has turned Michigan into a lifestyle brand.

When I was growing up in the 1990s, the major state tourism campaign was the more prosaic "Say Yes to Michigan," which made it seem like the state was a proposition to vote for at the next midterm election. The campaign came about in the 1970s, when deindustrialization left Michigan with the highest unemployment rate in the country, and young people fled in droves to seek work elsewhere. (Ironically, that slogan is now best remembered by people of my generation as the title of a song by Sufjan Stevens, who left the state for Brooklyn.) While the state's economy has stabilized somewhat since that nadir, Michigan has been unable to prevent its educated youth from leaving. It is one of only four states in the nation that has fewer college graduates now than it did ten years ago.

I've long suspected that the Pure Michigan campaign owes

its success, in part, to reaching those exiles—the state's prodigal children. A friend of mine, who spent her twenties working a high-stress job at an advertising firm in Chicago, told me that on especially bad days, after an hour-long commute back to her basement apartment, she would hole up in her bedroom with her laptop and watch the ads, one after another, and weep with homesickness.

"Carpools, conferences, microwave dinners," Allen intones. "They blur one into the next. We lose ourselves in the fog of everyday life, and drift away from what matters." This is perhaps the most popular of the campaign's television spots, "Lost and Found," focusing on Michigan's iconic lighthouses. It aired so frequently a few summers ago that I still know its copy by heart. According to Allen's dulcet tones, the "fog of everyday life"—the fog of late modernity—can be dispelled by "the light of more than one hundred lighthouses burning through that fog, and beckoning us back to what's real and true."

Michigan has recently been in the news for a more troubling kind of fog. In March 2016, *Newsweek* reported on toxic pollution in River Rouge, one of Detroit's southern industrial suburbs. The city is a bleak landscape of gas flares and smokestacks, and its air and water have been besieged by an unholy legion of chemicals: benzene, sulfuric acid, hydrochloric acid, methanol, and ammonia. The main culprits are two DTE Energy plants and a large steel factory. The plants are so dirty they regularly burnish the sky a deep orange hue and emit so many asthma-inducing toxins that the neighborhood has spawned a bootleg market for cheap inhalers.

The story drew national attention in part because it came on the heels of the Flint water crisis, which President Obama

had declared a state of emergency in January. All the hor-
rific anecdotes coming out of Flint are by now well known:
the bureaucratic apathy, the government cover-ups. The water
was so polluted with lead that all children under the age of six
were declared poisoned, and a local pastor stopped using it for
baptisms.

In light of this, it's tempting to view the Pure Michigan ads
as a particularly Orwellian form of propaganda—or, at the very
least, a deft act of corporate whitewashing. The poetic irony has
not been lost on the residents of Michigan, some of whom have
made parody videos of the travel ads, focused on places like
Flint and Detroit. In the comments section of a local news site,
one resident offered up an acronym to describe "pure" Michigan under Governor Rick Snyder: "Pillaged, Upended, Raided,
Emaciated."

Both pollution scandals took place on the southeast side of
the state, a region that frequently makes the national headlines
for pollution, corruption, and crime; Pure Michigan lies conve-
niently elsewhere. Tim Allen is from the Detroit area and has
been an occasional booster for the city's revival, but when he
was asked whether the Pure Michigan ads could lure millennials back to the state, he diverted attention to the coastline. "You
have to show them some of the boardwalk, beach type of communities, like Saugatuck. And the National Cherry Festival in
Traverse City," he said. Unlike the old Say Yes campaign, which
appealed to a sense of political obligation, the Pure Michigan
ads ask only for aesthetic appreciation. If the children are to
return, it will not be to rebuild the state's moribund cities but
to retreat into its bucolic peripheries.

If the pollution scandals have failed to tarnish the Pure Michigan brand, it's because they don't in any way disrupt the foundational myth of the ads: that the world can be neatly divided

into two kinds of places. There are the fast-paced centers of industry and greed, where we are forced to do others' bidding, and there are the pastoral retreats where we can find ourselves and, perhaps, be forgiven. The dichotomy is implicit in the ads' many appeals to viewers who are blinded by the fog—real or metaphorical—that pervades our cities. "As life starts moving faster and faster," says Allen, "we need to make a choice: to move faster with it, or to step off every now and then."

This idea that one can simply "step off" the path of modernity and retreat into the wilderness bears a long lineage in the American imagination, from the transcendental creeds of *Walden* to the Romantic allure of primitivism in all its forms. In his formative history of Chicago, *Nature's Metropolis*, William Cronon notes that the Midwest has often been characterized by a false division between the Fair Country and the Dark City, "the one pristine and unfallen, the other corrupt and unredeemed." Late nineteenth-century novelists like Hamlin Garland, Frank Norris, and Robert Herrick wrote about the rite of passage by which young people would leave their rural homelands to find work in Chicago, amid the stale air, the smoke, and the slaughterhouses, only to find themselves longing for the purity of the lands of their youth. Because they were disconnected from the natural world, Cronon argues, it became necessary for these urban transplants to maintain the myth that it was possible to escape into the wilderness—and in doing so, exculpate themselves from the dirty business of modernity.

To believe in this myth, though, is to ignore the actual extent to which human activity reshapes the natural world. The Great Lakes, which provide drinking water to more than 40 million people, are hardly wellsprings of purity. Over the past decade, loopholes in the Clean Water Act have turned the waters of Lake Michigan into what one environmental report referred to as "a witch's brew of pollutants." Temperatures in the Great Lakes have been warming since the late 1990s, and environmentalists predict lower water levels, drought, and a decline in biodiversity.

There was a time when I loved the Pure Michigan ads because they mirrored the way the terrain of my childhood existed in my imagination. But when you live here year-round, it's difficult to sustain the illusion. You begin to notice things: the frequent beach closings due to *E. coli*, the toxic algal blooms that marbleize the shallows of lakes with neon green foam. When I was a child, Lake Michigan would freeze each winter far into the perceivable distance. The ice covered more than half the lake and was thick enough that you could walk for miles toward the horizon, from which vantage the entire Earth resembled the tundra of Antarctica or the surface of the moon. This past winter, only a thin lip of ice extended over the shoreline and was gone by early February.

Unlike the scandals in Flint and Detroit, which can be pinned on corruption and corporate greed, reports about drought and dead zones point to no clear villain. It's difficult to read about them without feeling implicated. Still, these observable fluctuations are subtle, and it's easy to dismiss them as the product of El Niño, or the meteorological fickleness that has always characterized this part of the country. As summer approaches, there are still days when the landscape resembles the image of itself reflected in the Pure Michigan ads, when sunrise finds the beaches empty and the water along the shoreline a serene and crystalline blue. In the light of a glorious morning, it's tempting to believe that this is a place set apart: that the water itself is redemptive, that it will make us clean.

2016, The Awl

GHOST IN THE CLOUD

"I do plan to bring back my father," Ray Kurzweil says. He is standing in the anemic light of a storage unit, his frame dwarfed by towers of cardboard boxes and oblong plastic bins. He wears tinted eyeglasses. He is in his early sixties, but something about the light or his posture makes him seem older. Kurzweil is now a director of engineering at Google, but this documentary was filmed in 2009, back when it was still possible to regard him as a lone visionary with eccentric ideas about the future. The boxes in the storage unit contain the remnants of his father's life: photographs, letters, newspaper clippings, and financial documents. For decades, he has been compiling these artifacts and storing them in this sepulcher he maintains near his house in Newton, Massachusetts. He takes out a notebook filled with his father's handwriting and shows it to the camera. His father passed away in 1970, but Kurzweil believes that, one day, artificial intelligence will be able to use the memorabilia, along with DNA samples, to resurrect him. "People do live on in our memories, and in the creative works they leave behind," he muses, "so we can gather up all those vibrations and bring them back, I believe."

Technology, Kurzweil has conceded, is still a long way from bringing back the dead. His only hope of seeing his father resurrected is to live to see the singularity—the moment when computing power reaches an "intelligence explosion." At this point, according to transhumanists such as Kurzweil, people who are merged with this technology will undergo a radical transformation. They will become posthuman: immortal, limitless, changed beyond recognition. Kurzweil predicts this will happen by the year 2045. Unlike his father, he, along with those of us who are lucky enough to survive into the middle of this century, will achieve immortality without ever tasting death.

But perhaps the apostle Paul put it more poetically: "We shall not all sleep, but we shall all be changed."

I first read Kurzweil's 1999 book, *The Age of Spiritual Machines*, in 2006, a few years after I dropped out of Bible school and stopped believing in God. I was living alone in Chicago's southern industrial sector and working nights as a cocktail waitress. I was not well. Beyond the people I worked with, I spoke to almost no one. I clocked out at three each morning, went to after-hours bars, and came home on the first train of the morning, my head pressed against the window so as to avoid the specter of my reflection appearing and disappearing in the blackened glass. When I was not working, or drinking, time slipped away from me. The hours before my shifts were a wash of benzo breakfasts and listless afternoons spent at the kitchen window, watching seagulls circle the landfill and men hustling dollies up and down the docks of an electrical plant.

At Bible school, I had studied a branch of dispensational theology that divided all of history into successive stages by which God revealed his truth: the Dispensation of Innocence, the Dispensation of Conscience, the Dispensation of Human Government . . . We were told we were living in the Dispensation of Grace, the penultimate era, which precedes that glorious culmination, the Millennial Kingdom, when the clouds part and Christ returns and life is altered beyond comprehension. But I no longer believed in this future. More than the death of God, I was mourning the dissolution of this teleological narrative, which envisioned all of history as an arc bending assuredly toward a moment of final redemption. It was a loss that had fractured even my subjective experience of time. My hours had become non-hours. Days seemed to unravel and circle back on themselves.

The Kurzweil book belonged to a bartender at the jazz club where I worked. He was a physics student who whistled Steely Dan songs while counting his register and constantly jotted equations on the backs of cocktail napkins. He lent me the book a couple of weeks after I'd seen him reading it and asked—more out of boredom than genuine curiosity—what it was about. ("Computers," he'd replied, after an unnaturally long pause.) I read the first pages on the train home from work, in the gray and spectral hours before dawn. "The twenty-first century will be different," Kurzweil wrote. "The human species, along with the computational technology it created, will be able to solve age-old problems . . . and will be in a position to change the nature of mortality in a postbiological future."

Kurzweil had his own historical narrative. He divided all

of evolution into successive epochs: the Epoch of Physics and Chemistry, the Epoch of Biology and DNA, the Epoch of Brains. We were living in the fifth epoch, when human intelligence begins to merge with technology. Soon we would reach the singularity, the point at which we would be transformed into what Kurzweil called "spiritual machines." We would transfer or "resurrect" our minds onto supercomputers, allowing us to live forever. Our bodies would become incorruptible, immune to disease and decay, and we would acquire knowledge by uploading it to our brains. Nanotechnology would allow us to remake Earth into a terrestrial paradise, and then we would migrate to space, terraforming other planets. Our powers, in short, would be limitless.

It's difficult to account for the totemic power I ascribed to the book. Its cover was made from some kind of holographic material that shimmered with unexpected colors when it caught the light. I carried it with me everywhere, tucked in the recesses of my backpack, though I was paranoid about being seen with it in public. It seemed to me a work of alchemy or a secret gospel. It's strange, in retrospect, that I was not more skeptical of these promises. I'd grown up in the kind of millenarian sect of Christianity where pastors were always throwing out new dates for the Rapture. But Kurzweil's prophecies seemed different because they were bolstered by science. Moore's law held that computer processing power doubled every two years, meaning that technology was developing at an exponential rate. Thirty years ago, a computer chip contained 3,500 transistors. Today it has more than one billion. By 2045, the technology would be inside our bodies, and the arc of progress would curve into a vertical line.

Many transhumanists like Kurzweil contend that they are carrying on the legacy of the Enlightenment—that theirs is a philosophy grounded in reason and empiricism, even if they do lapse occasionally into metaphysical language about "transcendence" and "eternal life." As I read more about the movement, I learned that most transhumanists are atheists who, if they engage at all with monotheistic faith, defer to the familiar antagonisms between science and religion. Many regard Christianity in particular with hostility and argue that Christians are the greatest obstacle to the implementation of their ideas. In his novel, *The Transhumanist Wager* (2013), Zoltan Istvan, the founder of the Transhumanist political party, imagines Christians will be the ones to oppose the coming cybernetic revolution. Few Christians have shown much interest in transhumanism (or even awareness of it), but the Religious Right's record of opposing stem cell research and genetic engineering suggests it would resist technological modifications to the body. "The greatest threat to humanity's continuing evolution," writes transhumanist Simon Young, "is theistic opposition to Superbiology in the name of a belief system based on blind faith in the absence of evidence."

Though few transhumanists would likely admit it, their theories about the future are a secular outgrowth of Christian eschatology. The word "transhuman" first appeared not in a work of science or technology but in Henry Francis Cary's 1814 translation of Dante's *Paradiso*, the final book of the *Divine Comedy*. Dante has completed his journey through Paradise and is ascending into the spheres of heaven when his human flesh is suddenly transformed. He is vague about the nature of his new body. In fact, the metamorphosis leaves the poet, who has hardly paused for breath over the span of some sixty cantos, speechless. "Words may not tell of that transhuman change."

Dante, in this passage, is dramatizing the resurrection, the moment when, according to Christian prophecies, the dead will rise from their graves and the living will be granted immortal flesh. There is a common misunderstanding today that the Christian's soul is supposed to fly up to heaven after death, but the resurrection described in the New Testament is a mass, one-time eschatological event. For centuries, Christians believed that everyone who had ever died was being held in their graves in a state of suspended animation, waiting to be resuscitated at the Resurrection. The apostle Paul—who believed he would live to see the day—describes it as the moment when God "will transform our lowly bodies so that they will be like his glorious body." Much later, Augustine meditated on the "universal knowledge" that would be available to resurrected man: "Think how great, how beautiful, how certain, how unerring, how easily acquired this knowledge then will be." According to the prophecies, Earth itself would be "resurrected," returned to its prelapsarian state. The curses of the fall—death and degeneration—would be reversed and all would be permitted to eat from the tree of life, granting immortality.

The vast majority of Christians throughout the ages have believed these prophecies would happen supernaturally. God would bring them about, when the time came. But since the medieval period, there has also persisted a tradition of Christians who believed that humanity could enact the resurrection through material means: namely, through science and technology. The first efforts of this sort were taken up by alchemists. Roger Bacon, a thirteenth-century friar who is often considered the first Western scientist, tried to develop an elixir of life that would mimic the effects of the resurrection as described in Paul's epistles. The potion would make humans "immortal" and "uncorrupted," granting them the four dowries that would infuse the resurrected body: *claritas* (luminosity), *agilitas* (travel at the speed of thought), *subtilitas* (the ability to pass through physical matter), and *impassibilitas* (strength and freedom from suffering).

The Enlightenment failed to eradicate projects of this sort. If anything, modern science provided more varied and creative ways for Christians to envision these prophecies. In the late nineteenth century, a Russian Orthodox ascetic named Nikolai Fedorov was inspired by Darwinism to argue that humans could direct their own evolution to bring about the resurrection. Up to this point, natural selection had been a random phenomenon, but now, thanks to technology, humans could intervene in this process. "Our body," as he put it, "will be our business." He suggested that the central task of humanity should be resurrecting everyone who had ever died. Calling on biblical prophecies, he wrote: "This day will be divine, awesome, but not miraculous, for resurrection will be a task not of miracle but of knowledge and common labor." He speculated that technology could be harnessed to return Earth to its Edenic state. Space travel was also necessary, since as Earth became more and more populated by the resurrected dead, we would have to inhabit other planets.

Fedorov had ideas about how science could enact the resurrection, but the details were opaque. The universe, he mused, was full of "dust" that had been left behind by our ancestors, and one day scientists would be able to gather up this dust to reconstruct the departed. Another option he floated was hereditary resurrection: sons and daughters could use their bodies to resurrect their parents, and the parents, once reborn, could bring back their own parents. Despite the archaic wording, it's difficult to ignore the prescience underlying these ideas. Ancestral "dust" anticipates the discovery of DNA. Hereditary resurrection prefigures genetic cloning.

This theory was carried into the twentieth century by Pierre Teilhard de Chardin, a French Jesuit paleontologist who, like Fedorov, believed that evolution would lead to the Kingdom of God. In 1949, Teilhard proposed that in the future all machines would be linked to a vast global network that would enable human minds to merge. Over time, this unification of consciousness would lead to an intelligence explosion—the Omega point—enabling humanity to "break through the material framework of Time and Space" and merge seamlessly with the divine. The Omega point is an obvious precursor to Kurzweil's singularity, but in Teilhard's mind, it was how the biblical resurrection would take place. Christ was guiding evolution toward a state of glorification so that humanity could finally merge with God in eternal perfection. By this point, humans would no longer be human. Perhaps the priest had Dante in mind when he described these beings as "some sort of Trans-Human at the ultimate heart of things."

Transhumanists have acknowledged Teilhard and Fedorov as forerunners of their movement, but the religious context of their ideas is rarely mentioned. Most histories of the movement attribute the first use of the term "transhumanism" to Julian Huxley, the British eugenicist and close friend of Teilhard's who, in the 1950s, expanded on many of the priest's ideas in his own writings—with one key exception. Huxley, a secular humanist, believed that Teilhard's visions need not be grounded in any larger religious narrative. In 1951, he gave a lecture that proposed a nonreligious version of the priest's ideas. "Such a broad philosophy," he wrote, "might perhaps be called, not Humanism, because that has certain unsatisfactory connotations, but Transhumanism. It is the idea of humanity attempting to overcome its limitations and to arrive at fuller fruition."

The contemporary iteration of the movement arose in San Francisco in the late 1980s among a band of tech-industry people with a libertarian streak. They initially called themselves Extropians and communicated through newsletters and at annual conferences. Kurzweil was one of the first major thinkers to bring these ideas into the mainstream and legitimize them for a wider audience. His ascent in 2012 to a director of engineering position at Google heralded, for many, a symbolic merger between transhumanist philosophy and the clout of major technological enterprise. Transhumanists today wield enormous power in Silicon Valley—entrepreneurs such as Elon Musk and Peter Thiel identify as believers—where they have founded think tanks like Singularity University and the Future of Humanity Institute. The ideas proposed by the pioneers of the movement are no longer abstract theoretical musings but are being embedded into emerging technologies at places like Google, Apple, Tesla, and SpaceX.

Losing faith in God in the twenty-first century is an anachronistic experience. You end up contending with the kinds of things the West dealt with more than a hundred years ago: materialism, the end of history, the death of the soul. During the early years of my faithlessness, I read a lot of existentialist novels, filling their margins with empathetic exclamation points. "It seems to me sometimes that I do not really exist, but that I merely imagine I exist," muses the protagonist of André Gide's *The Counterfeiters.* "The thing that I have the greatest difficulty in believing in, is my own reality." When I think back on that period of my life, what I recall most viscerally is an unnameable sense of dread—an anxiety that would appear without warning and expressed itself most frequently on the landscape of my body. There were days I woke in a panic, certain that I'd lost some essential part of myself in the fume of a blackout, and would work my fingers across my nose, my lips, my eyebrows, and my ears until I assured myself that everything was intact. My body had become strange to me; it seemed insubstantial. I went out of my way to avoid subway grates because I believed I could slip through them. One morning, on the train home from work, I became convinced that my flesh was melting into the seat.

At the time, I would have insisted that my rituals of self-abuse—drinking, pills, the impulse to put my body in danger in ways I now know were deliberate—were merely efforts to escape; that I was contending, however clumsily, with the overwhelming despair at the absence of God. But at least one piece of that despair came from the knowledge that my body was no longer a sacred vessel; that it was not a temple of the Holy Spirit, formed in the image of God and intended to carry me into eternity; that my body was matter, and any harm I did to it was only aiding the unstoppable process of entropy for which it was destined. To confront this reality after believing otherwise is to experience perhaps the deepest sense of loss we are capable of as humans. It's not just about coming to terms with the fact that you will die. It has something to do with suspecting there is no difference between your human flesh and the plastic seat of the train. It has to do with the inability to watch your reflection appear and vanish in a window without coming to believe you are identical with it.

What makes the transhumanist movement so seductive is that it promises to restore, through science, the transcendent hopes that science itself obliterated. Transhumanists do not believe in the existence of a soul, but they are not strict materialists, either. Kurzweil claims he is a "patternist," characterizing consciousness as the result of biological processes, "a pattern of matter and energy that persists over time." These patterns, which contain what we tend to think of as our identity, are currently running on physical hardware—the body—that will one day give out. But they can, at least in theory, be transferred onto nonbiological substrata: supercomputers, robotic surrogates, or human clones. A pattern, transhumanists would insist, is not the same as a soul. But it's not difficult to see how it satisfies the same longing. At the very least, a pattern suggests that there is, embedded in the meat of our bodies, some spark that remains unspoiled even as our body ages; that there is some essential core of our being that will survive and perhaps transcend the inevitable degradation of flesh.

Of course, mind uploading has spurred all kinds of philosophical anxieties. If the pattern of your consciousness is transferred onto a computer, is the pattern "you" or a simulation of your mind? Another camp of transhumanists have argued that Kurzweil's theories are essentially dualistic, and that the mind cannot be separated from the body. You are not "you" without your fingernails and your gut bacteria. Transhumanists of this faction insist that resurrection can happen only if it is *bodily* resurrection. They tend to favor cryonics and bionics, which promise to resurrect the entire body or else supplement the living form with technologies to indefinitely extend life.

It is perhaps not coincidental that an ideology that grew out of Christian eschatology would come to inherit its philosophical problems. The question of whether the resurrection would be corporeal or merely spiritual was an obsessive point of debate among early Christians. One faction, which included the

Gnostic sects, argued that only the soul would survive death; another insisted that the resurrection was not a true resurrection unless it revived the body. For these latter believers—whose view would ultimately become orthodox—Christ served as the model. Jesus had been brought back in the flesh, which suggested that the body was a psychosomatic unit. In contrast to Hellenistic philosophy, in which the afterlife would be purely spiritual, Christians came to believe that the soul was inseparable from the body. In one of the most famous treatises on the resurrection, the theologian Tertullian of Carthage wrote: "If God raises not men entire, He raises not the dead. . . . Thus our flesh shall remain even after the resurrection."

Transhumanists, in their eagerness to preempt charges of dualism, tend to sound an awful lot like these early church fathers. Eric Steinhart, a "digitalist" philosopher at William Paterson University, is among the transhumanists who insist the resurrection must be physical: "Uploading does not aim to leave the flesh behind," he writes; "on the contrary, it aims *at the intensification of the flesh.*" The irony is that transhumanists are arguing these questions as though they were the first to consider them. Their discussions give no indication that these debates belong to a theological tradition that stretches back to the earliest centuries of the Common Era.

While the effects of my deconversion were often felt physically, the root causes were mostly cerebral. My doubts began in earnest during my second year at Bible school, after I read *The Brothers Karamazov* and entertained, for the first time, the implications of the classic theodicies—the problem of hell, how evil could exist in a world created by a benevolent God.

In our weekly dormitory prayer groups, my classmates would assure me that all Christians struggled with these questions, but the stakes in my case were higher because I was planning to join the mission field after graduation. I nodded deferentially as my friends supplied the familiar apologetics, but afterward, in the silence of my dorm room, I imagined myself evangelizing a citizen of some remote country and crumbling at the moment she pointed out those theological contradictions I myself could not abide or explain.

Still, mine was a glacial severance from the faith. I knew other people who had left the church, and was amazed at how effortlessly they had seemed to cast off their former beliefs, immersing themselves instead in the pleasures of epicureanism or the rigors of humanitarian work. Perhaps I clung to the faith because, despite my doubts, I found—and still find—the fundamental promises of Christianity beautiful, particularly the notion that human existence ultimately resolves into harmony. What I could not reconcile was the idea that an omnipotent and benevolent God could allow for so much suffering. I agreed with Ivan Karamazov that even the final moment of glorification could never cancel out the pain and anguish it was meant to redeem.

Transhumanism offered a vision of redemption without the thorny problems of divine justice. It was an evolutionary approach to eschatology, one in which humanity took it upon itself to bring about the final glorification of the body and could not be blamed if the path to redemption was messy or inefficient. Within months of encountering Kurzweil, I became totally immersed in transhumanist philosophy. By this point, it was early December and the days had grown dark. The city was besieged by a series of early winter storms, and snow piled up on the windowsills, silencing the noise outside. I increasingly spent my afternoons at the public library, researching things like nanotechnology and brain-computer interfaces.

Once, after following link after link, I came across a paper called "Are You Living in a Computer Simulation?" It was written by the Oxford philosopher and transhumanist Nick Bostrom, who used mathematical probability to argue that it's "likely" that we currently reside in a Matrix-like simulation of the past created by our posthuman descendants. Most of the paper consisted of esoteric calculations, but I became rapt when Bostrom started talking about the potential for an afterlife. If we are essentially software, he noted, then after we die we might be "resurrected" in another simulation. Or we could be "promoted" by the programmers and brought to life in base reality. The theory was totally naturalistic—all of it was possible without any appeals to the supernatural— but it was essentially an argument for intelligent design. "In some ways," Bostrom conceded, "the posthumans running a simulation are like gods in relation to the people inhabiting the simulation."

It began as an abstract theological preoccupation. I didn't think it was likely we were living in a simulation, but I couldn't help musing about how the classic theodicies I'd struggled with in Bible school would play out in a simulated cosmology. I thought I had put these problems to rest, but that winter they burbled back to the surface. It would happen unexpectedly. One moment I'd be waiting for the bus or doodling on a green guest-check pad during the slow hours of my shift; the next, I'd be rehashing Pascal, Leibniz, and Augustine, inserting into their arguments the term "programmers" instead of "God." I wondered: Could the programmers be said to be omniscient? Omnipotent? Benevolent? Computers got bugs that eluded even their creators. What if evil was nothing more than a glitch in the Matrix? Christian theology relied on a premise of divine perfection; God himself was said to be perfect, and he was capable, in theory, of creating a perfect universe. But what if our creator was just a guy in a lab running an experiment? The novelist John Barth, I recalled, had once jokingly mused that the universe was a doctoral candidate's dissertation, one that would earn its author a B-.

One afternoon, deep in the bowels of an online forum, I discovered a link to a cache of "simulation theology"—articles written by fans of Bostrom's theory. According to the "Argument for Virtuous Engineers," it was reasonable to assume that our creators were benevolent because the capacity to build sophisticated technologies required "long-term stability" and "rational purposefulness." These qualities could not be cultivated without social harmony, and social harmony could be achieved only by virtuous beings. The articles were written by software engineers, programmers, and the occasional philosopher. Some appeared on personal blogs. Others had been published in obscure, allegedly peer-reviewed journals whose interests lay at the intersection of philosophy, technology, and metaphysics.

I also found articles proposing how one should live in order to maximize the chances of resurrection. Try to be as interesting as possible, one argued. Stay close to celebrities, or become a celebrity yourself. The more fascinating you are, the more likely the programmers will hang on to your software and resurrect it. This was sensible advice, but it presumed the programmer was a kind of deist's God who set the universe in motion and then sat back to watch and be entertained. Was it not just as probable that the programmer had a distinct moral agenda, and that he punished or rewarded his simulated humans based on their adherence to this code? Or that he might even intervene in the simulation? The deeper I got into the articles, the more unhinged my thinking became. One day, it occurred to me: perhaps God *was* the designer and Christ his digital avatar, and the incarnation his way of entering the simulation to share tips about our collective survival as a species. Or maybe the creation of our world was a competition, a kind of video game in which each participating programmer invented one of the world religions, sent down his own prophet-avatar, and received points for every new convert.

By this point I'd passed beyond idle speculation. A new, more pernicious thought had come to dominate my mind: transhumanist ideas were not merely similar to theological concepts but could in fact *be* the events described in the Bible. It was only a short time before my obsession reached its culmination. I got out my old study Bible and began to scan the prophetic literature for signs of the cybernetic revolution. I began to wonder whether I could pray to beings outside the simulation. I had initially been drawn to transhumanism because it was grounded in science. In the end, I became consumed with the kind of referential mania and blind longing that animates all religious belief.

I've since had to distance myself from prolonged meditation on these topics. People who once believed, I've been told, are prone to recidivism. Over the past decade, as transhumanism has become the premise of Hollywood blockbusters and a passable topic of small talk among people under forty, I've had to excuse myself from conversations, knowing that any mention of simulation theory or the noosphere can send me spiraling down the gullet of that techno-theological rabbit hole.

This is not to say that I have outgrown those elemental desires that drew me to transhumanism—just that they express themselves in more conventional ways. Over the intervening years, I have given up alcohol, drugs, sugar, and bread. On any given week, my Google search history is a compendium of cleanse recipes, high-intensity workouts, and the glycemic index of various exotic fruits. I spend my evenings in the concrete and cavernous halls of a university athletic center, rowing across virtual rivers and cycling up virtual hills, guided by the voice of my virtual trainer, Jessica, who came with an app that I bought. It's easy enough to justify these rituals of health optimization as more than mere vanity, especially when we're so frequently told that physical health determines our mental and emotional well-being. But if I'm honest with myself, these pursuits have less to do with achieving a static state of well-being than with the thrill of possibility that lies at the root of all self-improvement: the delusion that you are climbing an endless ladder of upgrades and solutions. The fact that I am aware of this delusion has not weakened its power over me. Even as I understand the futility of the pursuit, I persist in an almost mystical belief that I can, through concerted effort, feel better each year than the last, as though the trajectory of my life led toward not the abyss but some pinnacle of total achievement and solution, at which point I will dissolve into pure energy. Still, maintaining this delusion requires a kind of willful vigilance that can be exhausting.

I was in such a mood last spring when a friend of mine from Bible school, a fellow apostate, sent me an email with the title "robot evangelism." "I seem to recall you being into this stuff," he said. There was a link to an episode of *The Daily Show* that had aired a year ago. The video was a satiric report by the correspondent Jordan Klepper called "Future Christ." The gist was that a Florida pastor, Christopher Benek, believed that in the future AI could be evangelized and brought to salvation just like humans.

"How does a robot become Christian?" Klepper asked.

"We're not talking about a Roomba or your iPhone," Benek replied. "We're talking about something that's exponentially more intelligent than we are." He was young for a pastor—late thirties, maybe even younger. He wore a navy blazer and was sweating liberally beneath the studio lights.

"You're saying that robots, given the ability to have higher thought, they will choose Christianity."

"Yeah," Benek replied. "I think it's a reasoned argument."

The segment ended with Klepper taking a telepresence robot around to different places of worship—a mosque, a synagogue, a Scientology booth—to see which religion it would choose. The interview had been heavily edited, and it wasn't really clear what Benek believed, except that robots might one day be capable of spiritual life, an idea that failed to strike me as intrinsically absurd. Pope Francis had recently declared his willingness to baptize aliens. These were strange times to be a man of the cloth, but at least people were thinking ahead.

I googled Benek. He had an MDiv from Princeton. He described himself in his bio as a "techno-theologian, futurist, ethicist, Christian transhumanist, public speaker, writer and tech pastor." He was also the founding chair of something called the Christian Transhumanism Association. I followed a link to the organization's website, which was professional looking but sparse. It included that peculiar quote from Dante: "Words cannot tell of that transhuman change." All this seemed unlikely. Was it possible there were now Christian Transhumanists? Actual believers who thought the Kingdom of God would come about through the singularity? All this time I had thought I was alone in drawing these parallels between transhumanism and biblical prophecy, but the convergences seemed to have gained legitimacy from the pulpit. How long would it be before everyone noticed the symmetry of these two ideologies—before Kurzweil began quoting the Gospel of John and Bostrom was read alongside the minor prophets?

I met with Benek at a café across the street from his church in Fort Lauderdale. In my email to him, I'd presented my curiosity as journalistic, unable to admit—even to myself—what lay behind my desire to meet. My grandparents live not too far from his church, so it was easy to pass it off as a casual excursion while visiting family, rather than the point of the trip itself.

He arrived in the same navy blazer he'd worn in *The Daily Show* interview and appeared just as nervous. Throughout the first half hour of our conversation, he seemed reluctant to divulge the full scope of his ideas, as though he was aware that he'd stumbled into an intellectual obsession that was bad for his career. *The Daily Show* had been a disaster, he told me. He had spoken with them for an hour about the finer points of his theology, but the interview had been cut down to his two-minute spiel on robots—something he insisted he wasn't even interested in; it was just a thought experiment he'd been goaded into. "It's not like I spend my days speculating on how to evangelize robots," he said.

The music in the café was not as loud as I would have liked. Several people nearby were flipping aimlessly at their phones in the manner of eavesdroppers trying to appear inconspicuous. I explained that I wanted to know whether transhumanist ideas were compatible with Christian eschatology. Was it possible that technology would be the avenue by which humanity achieved the resurrection and immortality?

I worried that the question sounded a little deranged, but Benek appeared suddenly energized. It turned out he was writing a dissertation on precisely this subject. The title was "The Eschaton Is Technological."

"Technology has a role in the process of redemption," he said. Christians today assume the prophecies about bodily perfection and eternal life are going to be realized in heaven. But the disciples understood those prophecies as referring to things that were going to take place here on Earth. Jesus had spoken of the Kingdom of God as a terrestrial domain, albeit one in which the imperfections of earthly existence were done away with. This idea, he assured me, was not unorthodox; it was just old.

I asked Benek about humility. Wasn't the gospel about the fallen nature of the flesh and our tragic limitations as humans?

"Sure," he said. He paused a moment, as though debating whether to say more. Finally, he leaned in and rested his elbows on the table, his demeanor markedly pastoral, and began speaking about the Transfiguration. This event, described in several of the Gospels, portrays Jesus climbing to the top of a mountain with three of his disciples. Suddenly, Moses and Elijah appear out of thin air, their bodies encircled with holy light. Then Jesus's appearance is changed. His disciples notice that "He was transfigured before them; and His face shone like the sun, and His garments became as white as light." Theologians have identified this as a moment when the temporal and the eternal overlapped, with Christ standing as the bridge between heaven and Earth.

It was a curious passage, Benek said. "Jesus is human, but he's also something else." Christ, he reminded me, was characterized by the hypostatic union: he was both fully human and fully God. What was interesting, he said, was that science had actually verified the potential for matter to have two distinct natures. Superposition, a principle in quantum theory, suggests that an object can be in two places at one time. A photon could be a particle, and it could also be a wave. It could have two natures. "When Jesus tells us that if we have faith nothing will be impossible for us, I think he means that literally."

By this point, I had stopped taking notes. It was late afternoon, and the café was washed in amber light. Perhaps I was a little dehydrated, but Benek's ideas began to make perfect sense. This was, after all, the promise implicit in the incarnation: that the body could be both human and divine, that the human form could walk on water. "Very truly I tell you," Christ had said to his disciples, "whoever believes in me will do the works I have been doing, and they will do even greater things than these." His earliest followers had taken this promise literally. Perhaps these prophecies had pointed to the future achievements of humanity all along, our ability to harness technology to become transhuman. Christ had spoken mostly in parables—no doubt for good reason. If a superior being had indeed come to Earth to prophesy the future to first-century humans, he would not have wasted time trying to explain modern computing or sketching the trajectory of Moore's law on a scrap of papyrus. He would have said, "You will have a new body," and "All things will be changed beyond recognition," and "On Earth as it is in heaven." Perhaps only now that technologies were emerging to make such prophecies a reality could we begin to understand what Christ meant about the fate of our species.

I could sense my reason becoming loosened by the lure of these familiar conspiracies. Somewhere, in the pit of my stomach, it was amassing: the fevered, elemental hope that the tumult of the world was authored and intentional, that our profound confusion would one day click into clarity and the broken body would be restored. Part of me was still helpless against the pull of these ideas.

It was late. The café had emptied and a barista was sweeping near our table. As we stood to go, I couldn't help feeling that our conversation was unresolved. I suppose I'd been hoping that Benek would hand me some final hermeneutic, or even offer a portal back to the faith, one paved by the certitude of modern science. But if anything had become clear to me, it was my own desperation, my willingness to spring at this largely speculative ideology that offered a vestige of that first religious promise. I had disavowed Christianity, and yet I'd spent the past ten years hopelessly trying to re-create its visions by dreaming about our postbiological future or fixating on the optimization of my own body—a modern pantomime of redemption. What else could lie behind these impulses but the ghost of that first hope?

Outside, the heat of the afternoon had cooled to a balmy warmth. I decided to walk for an hour along the streets of the shopping district, a palm-lined neighborhood along the canals of the Intracoastal from where you could glimpse the masts of the marina and, beyond them, the deep Prussian blue of the Atlantic. Fort Lauderdale is a hub for spring breakers, but it was only January and the city was still populated by the mon-eyed winter set. Argentineans and Chileans and French Canadi-ans spent all day at the beach and now, in these temperate hours before dusk, took to the streets in expensive-looking spandex. People jogged along the gauntlet of beachside boutiques and unfurled polyethylene mats beneath banyan canopies for yoga in the park. A flock of speed-bikers swooped along the shoulder and disappeared, leaving in their wake a faint gust of sweat.

I was thinking of the scene from *Hannah and Her Sisters* where Woody Allen's character, who spends the course of the film searching for the right religion, is in a morbid mood, walking along the footpaths of Central Park. "Look at all these people jogging," he scoffs, "trying to stave off the inevitable decay of the body." I have often felt this way myself when watching people exercise en masse, as though the specter of all those bodies in motion summed up the futility of the whole human project—or perhaps offered an unflattering reflection of my own pathetic striving. But on this particular evening, in the last light of day, there was something mesmerizing in the dance of all these bodies in space. There were old bodies and young bodies, men and women, their limbs tanned and lambent with perspiration. They were stretching and lunging with arms outstretched in a posture of veneration, all of them animated by the same eternal choreography, driven by the echo of that ancient hope. Perhaps it was, in the end, a hope that was rooted in delusion. But was it more virtuous to concede to the cold realities of materialism—to believe, as Solomon did, that we are sediment blowing aimlessly in the wind, dust that will return to dust?

The joggers swept past me on either side of the sidewalk and wove through the crowd, like particles dispersing in a vacuum. All of them were heading in the same direction, up the bridge that crossed the marina and ended at the spread of the ocean. I watched as they receded into the distance and disappeared, one by one.

2017, *n+1*

EXILED

It has become something of a commonplace to say that Mike Pence belongs to another era. He is a politician whom the *New York Times* has called a "throwback," a "dangerous anachronism," and "a conservative proudly out of sync with his times," a man whose social policies and outspoken Christian faith are so redolent of the previous century's culture wars that he appeared to have no future until he was plucked, in the words of one journalist, "off the political garbage heap" by Donald Trump and given new life. His rise to the vice presidency has marked the return of religion and ideology to American politics at a time when the titles of political analyses were proclaiming the "twilight of social conservatism" (2015) and the "end of white Christian America" (2016), and reveals the zombie-like persistence of the Religious Right, an entity that has been deemed moribund many times over and whose final demise was for so long considered imminent that even as white evangelicals came out in droves to support the Trump-Pence ticket, their enthusiasm was dismissed, in the *Washington Post*, as the movement's "last spastic breath."

But Pence is a curious kind of Christian politician. He is more fixated on theological arcana than on the Bible's greatest hits (the Ten Commandments, the Beatitudes). His faith is not that of Mike Huckabee, say, whose folksy Christian nationalism is reflected in the title of his book, *God, Guns, Grits, and Gravy*; nor is it the humble self-help Methodism to which George W. Bush once deferred (at least in his early years, before his faith was hijacked by a geopolitical crusade), speaking of Jesus as the guy who had "changed my heart." Indeed, the most peculiar thing about Pence's Christianity is how rarely he mentions Christ. Despite his fluency with scripture, he seldom quotes the Gospels. He speaks fondly not just of "the Good Book" but also of "the Old Book," by which he usually means the Hebrew Bible, and it is this earlier testament that he draws from in his speeches, often with the preface that it contains "ancient truths" that are "as true today as they were in millennia past."

Pence does indeed live in the past, a past far more ancient than anyone has assumed. He speaks of the Old Testament as familiar terrain and regards its covenants as deeply relevant to evangelicals like himself. The God of these stories is not the familiar, tranquilized Jesus of gospel hymns and dashboard figurines but the more forbidding Yahweh who disciplines and delivers the nation of Israel. The God of Abraham, Isaac, and Jacob—and the God of Mike Pence—is a God who sets up kings and tears them down, who raises up the poor from the dust and lifts the needy from the ash heap, who pulls candidates off the political garbage pile and allows them to rule with princes. He is a God who keeps his promises, and the promise, throughout the ages, has always been the same: that the chosen people will be restored to their rightful home.

The biblical concept of exile—a banishment followed by a return to the homeland—has lately acquired special meaning for evangelicals. The term inundated Christian discourse in the United States following the failure of the Religious Freedom Restoration Act (RFRA), which Pence, then the governor of Indiana, signed in 2015, soon after a judge struck down the state's ban on same-sex marriage. The bill, which would have allowed businesspeople such as florists and caterers to discriminate against gay clients, inspired a national boycott and culminated in a disastrous appearance on George Stephanopoulos's *This Week*, in which Pence evaded question after question and stammered about open-mindedness being a two-way street. "From people who preach tolerance every day," he said, "we have been under an avalanche of intolerance." Pence was forced to neuter the bill, and the ordeal soon fell out of the news cycle.

But for conservative Christians, who had long seen themselves at war with the culture, the backlash was a wake-up call. Rod Dreher, an Eastern Orthodox writer for *The American Conservative*, claims this was the moment he realized that American believers were "living in a new country." In late June 2015, the *Obergefell v. Hodges* decision legalized gay marriage in all fifty states, and Dreher proclaimed in *Time* magazine that the culture wars were officially over. Progressive views on marriage and sexuality had become consensus, and Christians would now be targeted as dissenters, their beliefs classed as hate speech. "We are going to have to learn how to live as exiles in our own country," he wrote. "We are going to have to learn how to live with at least a mild form of persecution." The same day, Russell

Moore, of the Southern Baptist Convention, lamented *Obergefell* but offered a brighter forecast, calling on Christians to "joyfully march toward Zion" as "strangers and exiles in American culture." Both Dreher and Moore went on to write books on the role of the church in an increasingly hostile culture, and soon, cries of exile (or #exile, per Twitter) could be heard all over Christendom.

I left the faith more than a decade ago but remain connected to it, tangentially, through a large born-again family and an abiding anthropological curiosity, so these things tend to reach me. I knew that while exile appeared to be a fluid metaphor—a way to talk about religious liberties and political impotence—it also had a specific historic referent: the period the Jews spent in Babylonian captivity. Accounts of the exile are scattered throughout the Old Testament, though the story generally begins in 587 BC, when Nebuchadnezzar's army razed Jerusalem and burned the Temple to the ground. The Israelites were deported to Babylon, where they remained for seventy years, lamenting the ruin of Zion and praying for deliverance. In these stories, the empire is led by a series of despotic rulers—Nebuchadnezzar, Nabonidus, Belshazzar—who seem to find sadistic pleasure in forcing the Jews to renounce their God and, when they refuse, throwing them to wild animals or into the fiery furnace. When I was studying theology at Moody Bible Institute—during the Bush years—none of the believers I knew were particularly drawn to these books. But Christians have returned to them during times of persecution, and apparently they had become newly relevant for believers who saw themselves as a religious minority in a hostile pagan empire—a people who had long mistaken Washington, D.C., for Jerusalem, and for whom the image of the White House lit up in a rainbow was a defeat as final as the desecration of the Temple.

Of course, for anyone familiar with evangelical rhetoric, it is obvious that "exile" is not a white flag but a revamped strategy. The Babylonian exile, after all, was temporary. All the lamentations were ultimately about deliverance, and that deliverance came in the form of a strongman: in 539 BC, Cyrus the Great, the king of Persia, conquered Babylon and allowed the Jews to return to Jerusalem.

Once Donald Trump became a serious contender for the Republican Party's presidential nomination in early 2016, some Christians saw him as the instrument of deliverance. This idea came primarily from the theological fringe that Trump courted during his campaign: televangelists, Pentecostals, health-and-wealth hucksters. It came from men like Lance Wallnau, an evangelical public speaker who met with Trump during his campaign and, in 2015, began writing articles that likened the candidate to Cyrus. Throughout history, Wallnau argued, God had used pagan leaders to enact his will and protect his people. Just as Cyrus was a powerful leader anointed by Yahweh to end the exile, so Trump was "a wrecking ball to the spirit of political correctness." Wallnau eventually published his theory in a book, *God's Chaos Candidate.* Just before the election, it reached number nineteen on Amazon's bestseller list.

Plenty of Christians cautioned against this narrative—most notably Moore, in the *Washington Post.* He and Dreher represent a more orthodox core of believers who remained skeptical of Trump and believed his presidency would be a continuation of pagan rule. (Dreher has condemned Christians who want to "Make Babylon Great Again.") This contingent was more likely to compare Trump to Nebuchadnezzar, a king who is not remembered kindly in the Old Testament. In one story, he decrees the construction of a gold statue of himself and orders his subjects to bow down and worship it. In another, his advisors fail to interpret his dream, and he threatens to kill off his entire court. He is suspicious of his advisors, tortured by nightmares of his own demise, slowly succumbing to madness. For Christians who were anti-Trump, the parallels were obvious and cause for concern. "There's another biblical figure who didn't acknowledge God, yet God used him to carry out a purpose," Dr. Alan Snyder, a Christian historian, wrote about Nebuchadnezzar on his blog. "His purpose? To destroy Jerusalem and take the people into captivity."

It was not immediately clear to me how Pence fit into these narratives. That summer, shortly after the Republican National Convention, a friend asked me about the likelihood of Pence solidifying the evangelical vote. (As a former believer, I am sometimes considered an authority on such things.) I remarked offhandedly that Christians regarded Pence as an intercessor, one who would temper the president's moral excesses just as Christ intervened two thousand years ago to mollify the reckless whims of Jehovah.

I'd forgotten that there is a more apt analogy in the Old Testament. One of the foremost heroes of the exile stories is Daniel, an Israelite who serves in Nebuchadnezzar's palace. Daniel manages to preserve his Jewish identity in the Babylonian court, refusing the king's food and wine and continuing to pray to his God, sometimes in secret. When Daniel correctly interprets one of the king's dreams, he is promoted to chief advisor, a position he uses to establish protections for the Jews and secure appointments for his Hebrew friends. He also ends up serving as the king's spiritual advisor, encouraging him to turn from idolatry and worship Yahweh, the one true God. Still, despite earning royal favor, Daniel frequently comes into conflict with the king's temper and the paganism of Babylon. When he refuses to obey a decree that would prohibit him from praying to his God, he is thrown into the lion's den.

These stories have long been read by Christians as a hand-book in civil disobedience. (Martin Luther King Jr. invoked the book of Daniel in "Letter from Birmingham Jail" to defend the virtue of protesting without a permit.) But the story of Daniel also suggests that godly people can negotiate power by influencing leaders whose values differ vastly from their own. At the dawn of the Trump era, the lesson contemporary evan-gelicals gleaned from the story of Daniel is that God's people can survive in exile—even under the fist of a despotic ruler—so long as one of their own tribe advocates on their behalf in the corridors of power.

College Park Church, the congregation that Mike Pence attended during his governorship, sits on a northern stretch of Indianapolis, among golf courses and mid-priced hotel chains. The neighborhood is on the cusp of the suburbs, many of which are named, incidentally, after the landscape of the Old Testa-ment: Lebanon, Carmel, Zionsville. As soon as I entered the foyer, I recognized it as the kind of church I grew up in: large and contemporary, but without the gaudy trappings of a mega-church; doctrinally orthodox, but passionate about social wel-fare. It's the kind of church that people like my parents would call "theologically sound," which is a way of saying that the pastors went to the right schools, that worship avoids the char-ismatic theater of snakes and spirit slaying, that the sermons never descend into partisan shilling. It is not, in short, the kind of church that is, or ever was, uniformly gung ho about Trump.

Pence took a somewhat circuitous route to evangelicalism.

He was raised Irish Catholic and converted in college, when he realized, at a Christian music festival, that "what happened on the cross, in some small measure, actually happened for me." He avoided explicitly linking his beliefs to his politics during his early public career, but his faith became deeper after he lost his second congressional race, in 1990. Shortly thereafter, he published an article in *Indiana Policy Review* called "Confessions of a Negative Campaigner," in which he swore off the smear tactics he had used in the past. The article began with the words of the apostle Paul in I Timothy 1:15: "Christ Jesus came to save sinners, among whom I am foremost of all."

In the 1990s, Pence began regularly attending an evangelical megachurch with his family and joined the board of the Indiana Family Institute, a far-right group that was antigay and antiabortion. By the time he campaigned again for Congress, in 2000, his faith was at the forefront of his platform, which zeroed in on issues such as abortion, school prayer, and support for Israel. When he arrived in Washington, his congressional aides often saw him reading his Bible. One staffer claimed that Pence would cite specific verses to justify policy decisions. ("These have stood the test of time," Pence said of the Scriptures. "They have eternal value.") His faith continued to inspire his political agenda as governor of Indiana. Throughout his tenure, he met with a small group of other Christian men who held themselves accountable as believers.

I was curious about Pence's spiritual heritage and how the Bible teaching he'd received had influenced his political worldview. But the more immediate reason I'd come to Indianapolis was that College Park was wrapping up an eighteen-month sermon cycle on exile. In the sanctuary, a dimmed auditorium with stadium seating, a churchgoer pointed to the spot a few rows behind me where Pence used to sit on Sunday mornings with his wife, Karen, taking copious notes while dressed in a windbreaker bearing the state seal. The last time this congregant had spotted Pence in church was shortly after he joined Trump on the Republican ticket. He was accompanied by two Secret Service agents and sneaked out before the benediction.

At that time, College Park's lead pastor, Mark Vroegop, was in the middle of the exile series. From early 2016 until the middle of 2017, he walked his congregation through Lamentations and Daniel, then on to a series called "This Exiled Life," concerned with the topic of religious liberties. These sermons drew on the Babylon stories to explore the kinds of ethical dilemmas that his congregants might encounter in the corporate world of boardrooms and watercoolers: Your boss hands down a new policy that your faith precludes you from fulfilling. Your co-workers don't know you're a Christian. Do you share your views or fly under the radar? "For some of you," Vroegop told his congregation, "the island of marginal Christianity is shrinking, and you're going to have to think very carefully, like you've never thought before. . . . Where do I draw the line?"

Vroegop is a tall, forty-something man with a commanding voice, the kind of pastor who seems equally suited to heading corporate leadership seminars. I met him one day in his office, a small, sunny room lined with hundreds of theology books, alphabetized by author. He gave me one of them—Timothy Keller's *Making Sense of God*—when I mentioned that I'd left the faith in my early twenties. He told me the sermons on exile grew out of conversations he had with his congregants following RFRA and the *Obergefell* decision. "I would encounter believers who, frankly, just had this sense of panic about them," he said. Many in his congregation, particularly those who worked in HR and higher education, were confronting new protocols about gender and sexuality at their jobs, and as he walked them through these situations, he realized that the Old Testament might be instructive. "I think in the Babylonian exile, there was this reality of, look, we're going to be here for a while, we've got to figure out how to be Jewish and to honor our God in the midst of a culture that is just godless," he said. "And there were folks who figured out how to do that. You know, Daniel gets to a very high level of government."

During the summer of 2016, Vroegop preached on the book of Daniel, describing Nebuchadnezzar as "an angry, irrational king" and likening Daniel's position to "the vice presidency, if you will, of the country." The sermons focused on the delicate balancing act that Daniel performs. While he strives to stay on the king's good side, he also tells him difficult truths and urges him to keep his promises to the exiles. He "dared to speak to kings who were filled with pride and idolatry," Vroegop said in one sermon. "Somehow, Daniel had figured out how to be faithful to God while serving the Babylonian empire faithfully as well." I pointed out to Vroegop what seemed obvious to me—that the sermons were an allegory about Pence and Trump. Vroegop listened patiently while I drew these parallels but insisted that Pence had not been on his mind when he preached. Pence, he said, wasn't even being considered at the time for the ticket. (Vroegop preached the final Daniel sermon on June 26; Pence was announced as running mate on July 15.)

Vroegop has a long-standing policy against speaking about Pence to the press, but others have floated the idea of Pence as a Daniel-like figure, including some Indianapolis Christians who know the vice president personally. Gary Varvel, a columnist and political cartoonist who has been friends with Pence since the nineties, published an op-ed last August in the *Indy Star* that compared Pence to Daniel, as well as to Joseph and Esther, Israelites who similarly "rose to the number two positions to ungodly kings in their day." When I talked to Varvel, he told me he'd thought of Daniel as soon as Pence was announced as Trump's running mate. He shared the theory with some Christian friends, who confessed that they had been thinking the same thing. Varvel hasn't spoken to him since he joined the campaign, but he suspects that Pence may have had these biblical stories in mind when he chose to partner with Trump. "I would be surprised if he didn't consider this as a divine appointment, so to speak," Varvel told me. Former Indiana secretary of state Ed Simcox, who once led Bible studies in the state legislature, echoed this sentiment in an interview with *World* magazine. When asked about Pence's decision to partner with Trump, Simcox replied, "Mike would be thinking about the role he can play for his country. How can I contribute? Mike could wind up as the foremost counselor to the king, like in the Bible."

It's clear that Pence sees himself as the defender of an imperiled religious minority, a mantle he assumed during the RFRA fallout. It's telling that throughout those appearances, Pence did not appeal to the country's supposed religious foundations; nor did he defer to Christian values as a normative national ethic. Instead, he declared that the law would "empower" religious people whose liberties were being "infringed upon," drawing on the grammar of identity politics. Pence is a politician who has tapped into the language of exile, and by the time he joined Trump's campaign, he had become fluent, promising James Dobson that a Trump-Pence administration "will be dedicated to preserving the liberties of our people, including the freedom of religion that's enshrined in our Bill of Rights." For Christians who were immersed in these ancient myths, Pence made for a familiar figure, a member of the tribe who would represent them in the court of a pagan empire, a man who could encourage an unpredictable king to keep his promises. A former advisor quoted in *GQ* claims that Pence joined the ticket after he was reminded that "proximity to people who are off the path allows you to help them get on the path."

If the stories of exile helped evangelicals come around to the idea of a Trump presidency, they have served a different purpose since Trump and Pence took office: they have been marshaled to incite loyalty to Trump—particularly within the administration itself. Ralph Drollinger, a former NBA player and founder of Capitol Ministries, leads Bible studies on Capitol Hill wherein "the Word of God is regularly explicated and applied in specific to the life of a Public Servant." The gatherings, which are known to insiders as the Members Bible Study, take place weekly in both the House and Senate. During the Obama administration, Pence was one of the Bible study's sponsors, along with Michelle Bachmann, Tom Price, and Mike Pompeo.

A few weeks after the 2016 election, on November 28, Drollinger held a reception where he distributed Bible-study notes on the stories of Daniel, Joseph, and Mordecai. He declined my request for an interview, but Capitol Ministries sent me the notes to this study, "Maintaining Biblical Attitudes with New Political Leadership," which was clearly designed to quell internal fractiousness over the incoming president. (Drollinger was an outspoken Trump supporter throughout the campaign.)

Drollinger's Bible study began by acknowledging that many people in office had been vocal about their displeasure at Trump's election. The point of the study was to demonstrate the "exemplary behavior" of Old Testament figures like Daniel, "who stood their ground for God, and yet maintained respect for those in authority with whom they did not agree." What distinguished Daniel, in Drollinger's estimation, was his "loyal service" to and "manifest respect" for the king. Despite the fact that he served a pagan ruler who did not recognize his religion, Daniel made himself useful and encouraged Nebuchadnezzar to follow scriptural commands. "We may not be able to interpret a king's dreams today," Drollinger wrote, "but we can put into words the ageless truths of God's Holy Writ!" According to the study, Daniel and biblical figures like him assiduously followed the commands of the kings they served and exhibited an attitude of general compliance ("Nor did they call their boss names in the media" read a tongue-in-cheek aside). He then explicitly likened Pence to Daniel. "For years, Governor Pence has embodied these aforesaid biblical characteristics, and God has elevated him to the number-two position in our government."

Pence has certainly fulfilled this prescription of loyalty. During the first full Cabinet meeting, the vice president declared that working for Trump was "the greatest privilege of my life," provoking a chain of obsequious echoes from the other attendees. His unwavering devotion to his leader has earned him the endearment "sycophant in chief." He has declined to publicly disagree with the president, even in the crucible of his worst political traumas. When Trump refused to condemn white supremacists in Charlottesville, Virginia, for example, Pence not only defended him but did so in the soothing tones of a spiritual advisor. "I know this president," he told Matt Lauer. "I know his heart."

And yet, it would be difficult to overstate how far Drollinger's exegesis—which imagines Daniel as a deferential subject— strays from Christian orthodoxy, which traditionally celebrates him as a righteous dissenter. (It's also worth mentioning that Daniel was a slave, so whatever loyalty he exhibited was, in fact, compulsory.) Pence's shows of deference, by contrast, reek of political strategy. His tenure so far reflects the more cynical implication of Drollinger's lesson: that the most expedient way to accomplish a religious agenda is to perform loyalty to the king while working diligently behind the scenes on behalf of your own people. Pence was instrumental in the choice of Neil Gorsuch for the Supreme Court and is believed to have influenced many Cabinet appointments, including those of Betsy DeVos, Tom Price, and Mike Pompeo—a cohort that, in the words of the writer Jeff Sharlet, may be "the most fundamentalist Cabinet in history." "Evangelicals have had an unbelievably open door with this administration," said Johnnie Moore, a public relations executive and member of the Trump campaign's evangelical advisory board, a group of Christian leaders who continue to counsel the president on spiritual matters. While Moore told me that Trump himself has strong ties to evangelicals, he emphasized Pence's deep relationships with leaders in the Christian community, and said that the vice president has opened the White House to his longtime friends. Christian lobbyists, along with Pence, played an important role in persuading Trump last December to declare that the United States would recognize Jerusalem as Israel's capital. In his address to the Knesset the next month, Pence explicitly tied American history to the Jewish exile narratives. "In the story of the Jews," he said, "we've always seen the story of America." Israeli Prime Minister Benjamin Netanyahu rounded out the metaphor when he visited the United States in March and joined the chorus of evangelical leaders who see Trump as a twenty-first-century incarnation of the heroic Persian king. "I want to tell you that the Jewish people have a long memory," he said to Trump in the Oval Office. "We remember the proclamation of the great King Cyrus the Great . . . twenty-five hundred years ago, he proclaimed the Jewish exiles in Babylon can come back and rebuild our temple in Jerusalem."

Although Pence has denied that he has higher ambitions, political commentators haven't ruled out the prospect of a Pence presidency. Last year, he launched the Great America Committee, the first PAC started by a sitting vice president. This development, coupled with reports that he was hosting dinners for wealthy Republican donors at his official residence, and his choice of a presidential campaign operative as his first chief of staff, led to rumors that he might be running a shadow campaign. Regardless of whether he ends up running in 2020— or whether some fateful event promotes him to commander in chief—it appears he is planning a political future independent of Trump, a prospect that causes no shortage of anxiety on the left. It is now something of a cliché to point out that Trump's erraticism and lack of moral center might actually be preferable to Pence's ideological determination. Sarah Jones remarked in *The New Republic* that if Pence had his way, America would become like Gilead, the dystopian state of Margaret Atwood's *The Handmaid's Tale*, where women are considered property and "gender traitors" are publicly executed.

But one needn't look to dystopian fiction to conjure the kind of theocracy that Pence might prefer. It's right there in the Bible. After the Israelites were freed from exile, they returned to Jerusalem, rebuilt the Temple, and constructed a wall around the city. Under the leadership of a high priest, Judah became a theological state operating according to the Law of Moses, which outlined an inflexible code of hygiene and diet and forbade divorce and homosexuality. Some Old Testament sources dramatize this era as a revival of religious and ethnic purity, a period in which Jerusalem was systematically purged of foreign influences; in the Book of Ezra, non-Jews were persecuted, and men were forced to give up their foreign wives and children.

Pence himself has alluded to this return narrative in his speeches and public appearances. The verse he chose for his swearing-in as vice president—II Chronicles 7:14—reiterates the conditions of God's covenant with Israel and the promise of a restored theocratic homeland. American evangelicals see themselves as the inheritors of these covenants, which is something commentators miss when they predict, again and again, the decline of the Religious Right. Such assumptions rest on the modern, liberal notion that history is an endless arc of progress and that religion, like all medieval holdovers, will slowly vanish from the public sphere. But evangelicals themselves regard history as the Old Testament authors do, as a cycle of captivity, deliverance, and restoration, a process that is sometimes propelled by unlikely forces—pagan strongmen, despotic kings. This narrative lies deep in the DNA of American evangelicalism and is one of the reasons it has remained such a nimble and adaptive component of the Republican Party.

One of Pence's favorite Bible verses is Jeremiah 29:11: "For I know the plans I have for you . . . plans to prosper you and not to harm you, plans to give you hope and a future." The verse, which currently hangs above the mantel of the vice president's residence in Washington, contains God's promise to free the Jews after their captivity in Babylon. In a later verse, God vows, "I will gather you from all the nations and places where I have banished you . . . and I will bring you back to the place from which I carried you into exile."

Kingdoms rise and kingdoms fall. After Cyrus conquered Babylon, the region remained within the Persian Empire until

331 BC, when it fell to the Greeks under Alexander the Great. The Romans came next, then the Arab Islamic empires, and the Ottomans. Today, several of the countries that once made up the Neo-Babylonian Empire—including Syria and Iraq—are blighted by war and political chaos as vicious as that of the biblical era. Since the beginning of the civil war in Syria, 11 million people have fled their homes. Many are living in exile across the Middle East, while others have sought refuge in Europe or the United States—a humanitarian crisis that, according to the UN Refugee Agency, is the worst since the Rwandan genocide.

In November 2015, days after the Paris terrorist attacks, Mike Pence, as governor, issued a directive suspending the resettlement of Syrian refugees in Indiana. He claimed this was a security measure, arguing that Syrian refugees had carried out the attacks. (The culprits were in fact believed to be EU citizens, though there were reports one had posed as a refugee.) Pastor Vroegop noted, during our conversation, that Indianapolis was home to a sizable refugee community. It was something he mentioned in passing, while describing the church's outreach programs, but it stuck with me. During my time at College Park, nobody said anything nativist or xenophobic; Vroegop himself spoke of the "growing, beautiful diversity" of his congregation. Still, it became increasingly difficult to ignore a central, nagging irony: that the rhetoric of exile had cleared the way for an administration that is waging war on actual political exiles—particularly those who come from the land of the Old Testament.

Before I left Indianapolis, I visited Exodus Refugee Immigration, the largest resettlement agency in the state. The offices occupy a large warehouse on the east side of the city, in one of those postindustrial neighborhoods that has an almost rural quietude—empty lots reverting to prairie, long shadows across vacant sidewalks. After Pence's 2015 Syrian ban, Exodus partnered with the American Civil Liberties Union, which believed that the ban was unconstitutional, to file a lawsuit against the governor. Eventually, an appeals court ruled that Pence's directive amounted to "discrimination on the basis of nationality." Cole Varga, the executive director of Exodus, told me that last year had been "fairly chaotic," which struck me as a morbid understatement. Because of the travel bans, Exodus had received roughly half the arrivals they had expected, and their federal funding had taken steep cuts; that February, he'd let go of more than a third of his staff.

Varga introduced me to Shereen, a Syrian exile whose journey to the United States was almost derailed by the travel ban in January 2017. She, her husband, and her son had been living in Turkey as refugees for four years when their file was finally referred to the United States. They were packed and ready to go when they got the news that their flight had been canceled. "We thought we would never get the chance to come," Shereen told me. "For my husband and I, it's not a problem. We can live anywhere, we can work. We can start all over. But we were more concerned for my son. . . . We wanted the opportunity to come to the United States to provide a life for him."

Her son, Jowan, was in the Exodus office with her. He was diagnosed with cerebral palsy at birth and is in a wheelchair. Shereen explained that from the time they fled Aleppo in 2013, Jowan hadn't been able to attend school or receive physical therapy. When a federal appeals court put the ban on hold, she and her family came to the United States, and Jowan is now enrolled in school and receiving treatment. But they are among the lucky ones. Varga told me that he spends a lot of time thinking about all the people who "should be here right now." When I asked what happened to the refugees who'd been barred by the travel bans, he said they were likely still in the camps. Once a refugee's file is allocated to the United States, he explained, it's stuck in that pipeline, and it would be rare for it to be transferred to a different country. "So they might just be sitting there—well, maybe forever."

Throughout our conversation, I kept thinking of a speech Pence gave a few months earlier at the Mayflower Hotel in Washington, at an event for persecuted Christians. He argued, as he has elsewhere, that Christians are called to live in exile, "outside the city gate," barred from the security of the polis. Even though this administration has returned evangelicals to power, Pence still refers to Christians as an endangered minority. "No people of faith today face greater hostility or hatred than the followers of Christ," he said in the speech. His sympathy for exiles, it seems, doesn't extend to those of other religions. Pence often pays lip service to the religious liberties of "all people of all faiths," but he has consistently defended Trump's measures to prevent Muslims from entering the United States. When Trump signed the travel ban that would have prevented Shereen and her family from immigrating, Pence stood by his side.

Though the vice president often draws from its promises of redemption, the Old Testament is undergirded by a brutal moral calculus that is often difficult to reconcile with the teachings of Christ. Israel always gets what it deserves—punishment or deliverance—and yet so many others are the collateral damage of that cycle. There are the enemies of Israel, who are slain without mercy. And there are the countless foreign tribes who get caught in the crosshairs—groups who are settled on territories God intends for Judah, or people whose religion poses a threat to Jewish purity. Their demise appears in the margins of these stories, often in a single sentence: "They burned all the towns where the Midianites had settled, as well as all their camps." I remember coming across these passages when I was in Bible school, struggling with the first shadows of doubt, trying and failing to understand why so many people had to suffer for one group's redemption—why this ongoing drama between the elect and their God had to come at such a terrible cost.

ACKNOWLEDGMENTS

I am incredibly grateful to Gerry Howard for his dedication to this book and for prompting me to write about Mike Pence; and to Matt McGowan for believing in this collection and helping it find a home. Many thanks to all the magazine and anthology editors who selected, contributed to, and published these pieces, including Robert Atwan, Emily Cooke, Eleanor Duke, Alex Halperin, David Haglund, Bill Henderson, Leslie Jamison, Silvia Killingsworth, Wendy Lesser, James Marcus, Stewart O'Nan, Jeramie Orton, Ladette Randolph, Dayna Tortorici, Michelle Wildgen, and Rachel Wiseman. I am especially indebted to Nausicaa Renner, without whose enthusiasm and encouragement many of these essays would not exist, and to Jon Baskin, who published some of the earliest pieces and whose editorial guidance has made my writing more expansive and more rigorous.

I've had the good fortune of learning from several writers whose instruction and mentorship has been invaluable, among them Fred Schafer in Chicago, as well as all the folks at the University of Wisconsin–Madison—especially Jesse Lee Kercheval, Ron Kuka, Anne McClintock, Judith Claire Mitchell, Lorrie Moore, and Rob Nixon. Many of these essays benefited from early readers who are also friends, most of whom live (or have lived, at one time) in Madison: Lydia Conklin, Krista Eastman, Zac Fulton, Alyssa Knickerbocker, Christopher Mohar, Hannah Oberman-Breindel, Marian Palaia, and Yuko Sakata. I cannot offer enough gratitude to my family for their enduring love and support; to Lisa Tomczak for her guidance and wisdom; and, above all, to my husband, Barrett Swanson, for everything.